Over the next twenty years
the emphasis
in management will be on the
understanding of decision making

—Peter Drucker

WINTHROP MANAGEMENT SERIES
William H. Brickner, *Series Editor*

Management Decisions:

A Behavioral Approach

Edward Sanford
Harvey Adelman

Winthrop Publishers, Inc.
Cambridge, Massachusetts

Library of Congress Cataloging in Publication Data

Sanford, Edward.
    Management decisions: a behavioral approach

(Winthrop management series)
    1. Decision-making.   2. Management.   I. Adelman, Harvey, joint author.
II. Title.
HD30.23.S25   658.4'03   76-58434
ISBN 0-87626-548-4

*To our students
for the help, for the trust,
for the good times shared*

Cover illustration by Ruth Williams.

Text illustrations by Dave Close.

contents

one

two

three

Please Read the Inside of Your Environment Carefully, Before Proceeding 51

four

Getting the Decision Straight 63

five

Who Will Riddle Me a Riddle of the How and Why of Hunches? 93

six

editor's preface

Energy crisis! Political crisis! Personal crisis! Economic crisis! . . . . I believe they all have a common element: *mismanagement*. It may be mismanagement of resources, mismanagement of everyday activities, mismanagement of organizations large and small, or mismanagement of societies in general; however, it is becoming increasingly clear that many people do not manage well.

If we define management as planning and using resources such as time, money, energy, etc. to attain stated objectives (goals), then the ability to manage well can have a significant impact on almost every life experience. We conceived the Winthrop Management Series with the idea that the basic skills and principles necessary for successful managing are not complicated; almost anyone can learn them. With a basic understanding of these skills and principles, people can become more effective managers at all levels: in large organizations, in small groups, or in their personal lives.

WHO NEEDS 'EM? (MORE BOOKS ON MANAGEMENT, THAT IS)

We have directed the books in this series primarily toward those people who would like to do a better job of managing, yet who have neither the time nor the inclination to enroll in a full program of management courses at the university level. The authors have written the books to be used individually, or as a set, in industrial training programs, community colleges, university extension classes, or as focused readings in undergraduate or graduate management courses. In addition, the authors hope that the books will provide useful self-study material for those people who learn on their own by reading daily.

Organizations in all areas of society are growing larger and more complex. As a result, individuals with a wide variety of backgrounds and vocations are recognizing the need to learn the principles of good management. Hopefully they can benefit from the Winthrop Management Series. Experienced professional managers also may see these volumes as an aid in successfully carrying out one of the most important managerial duties, that of helping subordinates to manage *their* jobs more effectively.

WHAT THIS SERIES IS ABOUT

The books in the series are concerned with those skills which experienced managers find most critical for developing a successful managerial career. The results of a nationwide

Skills		Personal Attributes	
Leadership and Motivation	18.7%*	Ability to Work with Others	22.5%*
Information Systems	11.6%	Drive, Energy	21.7%
Communication	11.2%	Adaptability to Change	11.9%
Understanding Human Behavior	10.8%	Intellectual Capacity	11.9%
Finance	10.4%	Ability to Communicate	10.4%
Awareness of Environment	7.1%	Integrity	8.4%
Planning	6.4%		

*Shows relative weight assigned from 100% total.

questionnaire to 266 top and middle managers in business, government, and nonprofit organizations are shown in the table on p. x. The managers ranked these skills and personal attributes as most important for long-term managerial success in the future.[1] Accordingly, the authors have examined many of these skills and attributes in these six series volumes:

1. *The Planning Process* by Brickner and Cope.
2. *Understanding Information Systems: Foundations for Control* by Campbell.
3. *Organizational Team Building* by Ends and Page.
4. *Communicating in Organizations* by Rockey.
5. *Management Decisions: A Behavioral Approach* by Sanford and Adelman.
6. *The Motivation Process* by Schaefer.

Communication, decision making, and the ability to motivate oneself and others are process skills important to all managers. The books on planning, organization building, and control through information systems include the most important functions that managers perform. Although the six books do not discuss all of the many topics involved in management, we feel that they cover the most important ones.

MAJOR SERIES THEMES

One of the main themes of the Winthrop Management Series is the concept of *systems* or *processes*. Management is not a series of unrelated activities. Like the universe, management is an interlocking rational system governed by "laws."

---

[1] Brickner, W.H. *The Managers of Today Look at Those of Tomorrow.* Presented at the National Meeting of the Academy of Management, Seattle, Wash., August, 1974.

The fact that many of these laws are "undiscovered" should not detract from the principle that management is an ongoing process. This process involves inputs of resources and information, the shape and form of which are changed, resulting in some outcome. Information about the outcome (feedback) is then compared with the desired outcome (objective). If the comparison is unsatisfactory, the inputs or the processor are changed. The following diagram illustrates this concept:

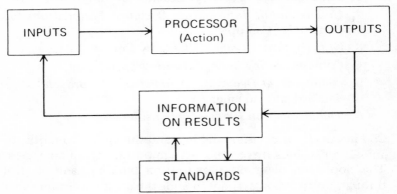

Each of the topics covered in this series is actually a smaller system, or process, that is a part of the overall system of management.

Another key concept in organizing the material for these books is *Pareto's Law*. This "law" states that a relatively small percentage of the inputs creates a large percentage of the outcomes. (For example, 20 percent of a firm's customers may be responsible for 80 percent of its sales volume.) With regard to the series, each author has organized each book around a few specific ideas which he or she believes to be the major keys for successfully mastering each basic process discussed.

The application of principles and theories to real-world situations is an extremely difficult problem for many people. To help bridge the gap between theory and practice, each volume contains a *Panel Discussion* of several successful management practitioners. They are individuals with varied backgrounds who in their careers have successfully used whatever management process they were talking about. The panelists addressed themselves to the problems and opportunities which could result from applying the theories discussed by the author in the preceding chapter of the book. The resulting dialogues are rich in insights and guides that can aid both novice and experienced managers.

ACKNOWLEDGMENTS

Many people have been involved in the creation of the Winthrop Management Series. However, one person above all made it possible. My personal gratitude goes to Michael Meehan, our editor at Winthrop Publishers, Inc. Mike provided early encouragement when the series was but a faint idea. Subsequently as this idea became more tangible, he was willing to "put his money where his mouth is" and support the publishing of the six volumes.

The help which these books will provide to managers is the result of the unstinting efforts of a creative team of authors and panelists, each of whom contributed to the series the knowledge of a lifetime of managerial experience. They all took time out from very busy professional lives to share this knowledge with others. My thanks to each of them.

William H. Brickner
Series Editor
Los Altos, California

authors' preface

I suppose that many people who will examine this little book will ask, "Why publish another book on decision making?" A fair question, indeed! In the past few years, hundreds of books on the subject have been increasing the size of book publishers' catalogues and the size of the textbook bill for students of business and management. Indeed, why another?

This is not a piece of research; nor is it a comprehensive tome but rather an attempt to look beyond the highly rationalistic "cookbook" approach to decision making that requires the manager to externalize his choices into a series of pseudo-sensible steps. It assembles a little data in the form of dialogues to find out what managers are actually doing. It emphasizes a synthesis of reason and intuition in decision making. But, most of all, it tries to look beyond what is happening today, to get a fresh perspective.

The first chapter defines the decision-making function. The second takes up the issue of whether decision making is intuitive or can be broken down into a series of steps that can be learned. In the third chapter, systematic decision making by the application of ideas from the field of "decision theory" are explored, and, briefly, the relevance of environment to the decision-making process. Chapter Four presents what we feel is a sensible model for this approach. Chapter Five deals directly with intuition in decision making—What is it? How does it work? How can it be developed?—while Chapter Six discusses the significance of decision-making "styles."

Since this book is in part an attempt to bridge a chasm
in thinking, we have many friends, colleagues, students, and
collaborators who have, deliberately or by default, assisted
in its development. So many people from disparate disciplines have aided us, it would be impossible to thank them all,
but our gratitude to our MBA students in Pepperdine University's School of Business and Management is overwhelming. The learning environment at the School is particularly
conducive to this type of sharing. As a matter of fact we have
discussed these concepts and ideas with so many businessmen
in our Master's Degree Programs at Pepperdine over the last
several years we can no longer determine who is responsible
for what part of the book. We are particularly grateful to the
seven panelists who generously gave of their time and talents
for the discussions in this book. Yet the burden of the responsibility for the approach must remain ours.

The authors would also like to acknowledge a special
thanks to Roberta Sanford for her help in preparing the
manuscript and to Dave Close, the talented artist who did the
graphic illustrations for the cartoons.

Los Angeles   Edward Sanford
                                                  Harvey Adelman

Management
Decisions:

one

Decisions. . . Decisions,
. . . Decisions!

Man's mind, stretched to a new idea,
never goes back to its original
dimension!

Oliver Wendell Holmes

LEARNING OBJECTIVES

When you have completed this chapter you should begin to understand the following:

1. Why decision making is essentially a problem in *cognition* or knowing and, as such, involves both awareness and judgment.
2. That decision making is a process that includes both the *collection* and *evaluation* of relevant information from surrounding data.
3. Why poor decisions always involve an implicit *opportunity loss*.
4. That making decisions is a *basic*, perhaps "the most basic," management skill.

GLOSSARY

Cognition This is a technical term borrowed from psychology that refers to the process of knowing something, including both the act of becoming aware of it and also the act of evaluating it.

Opportunity Loss Sometimes called opportunity cost, the term is borrowed from economics and refers to the foregone gains which could have been realized if a better decision had been made. For example, if the price of wheat is higher than the price of barley at harvest time, then the opportunity loss from a decision to grow barley is the lost revenue which would have resulted from a decision to grow wheat in the planting season.

DECISIONS... DECISIONS... DECISIONS

INTRODUCTION

One characteristic that makes people much more interesting than amoebas, at least to other people, is the ability to make sense out of the environment and to make fairly good decisions on the basis of hopelessly inadequate data. This trait seems to have evolved for the primary purpose of ensuring biological survival. It is of incalculable value in solving problems and making decisions.

This is a book about deciding! You may have already concluded that it is a waste of time to think about deciding. Perhaps you have even reached the conclusion that now you are satisfied with the way you make decisions, that it would be too difficult to try to improve the way you decide things. But, you see, you have to *decide* to accept those conclusions. And just how do you know those decisions are really sound?

How do *you* make decisions? Do you flip a coin? Ask a friend? Consult a fortune teller? You may, for the moment at least, be rather bored with the whole idea of mulling over the process you use in making choices; but what is completely obvious, though sometimes unappreciated, is the idea that every person, since early childhood, continuously faces new dilemmas, is continuously having to "figure out what went wrong or what to do," is continuously having, in short, to decide.

Whether a manager is involved in evaluating new opportunities or eliminating long-standing difficulties, decision making for management is essentially business problem solving. The process of deciding things is intimately related to the whole process of knowing, or what psychologists call cognition. This is true because knowing "what the problem is" will assist in deciding "what to do about it," that is, finding the best solution. Both problem solving and decision making consist of at least three phases:

1. Knowing or diagnosing the problem which necessitates a decision.
2. Singling out decision criteria or attributes relevant to the solution of the problem.
3. Evaluating alternative solutions and choosing a particular alternative which best meets the criteria.

THE FIRST MANAGERIAL SKILL

The process of knowing what to do, or deciding, is fundamental not only for individuals in their personal lives, but

DECIDING NOT TO DECIDE

" THE RESOLUTION BY THE ACTION COMMITTEE
TO TAKE DECISIVE STEPS WAS THEN TABLED UNTIL
THE NEXT MEETING."

also for professional managers. In fact, few skills involved
in the work of managing are as crucial; all of a manager's
other functions involve decisions of varying gravity. Peter

Drucker calls decision making the "first managerial skill."[1]
David W. Miller and Martin K. Starr refer to it as the "main
responsibility and function of the manager,"[2] and point out
further that the manager is "regarded and evaluated in terms
of success in making decisions":[3]

> The typical manager has other functions in addition
> to making decisions. He has to do many other things.
> But most organizations make continual attempts to
> relieve the manager of his more or less routine opera-
> tions so that he will have more time for the critical
> decision function.[4]

A manager's entire orientation is toward solving problems and making decisions rather than toward personally
performing the actions necessary for implementation; usually
the actions are carried out by others. A manager therefore
may be viewed as a professional knight-errant in the art of
deciding. Uncertainty and ambiguity are the monsters. Slay-
ing them are the quests. However, whether the outcome is
the result of wit, wisdom, or just plain luck, the ultimate
decision is undoubtedly the most creative and critical moment of truth in the process of managing. Why? The answer
is simple: mistakes are expensive! There is always an implied
opportunity loss associated with poor decision making. The
loss that results from a poor decision is precisely the foregone
gains, personal and organizational, which could have resulted
from a better choice.

Since the process of solving problems and making decisions is a key factor in both managerial and personal success, you might reasonably expect that we know a lot about

---

[1] Peter F. Drucker, *Management: Tasks, Responsibilities, Prac-
tices*, (New York: Harper and Row, Publishers, 1973), pp. 464–465.
[2] David W. Miller and Martin K. Starr, *The Structure of Human
Decisions*, (Englewood Cliffs, N.J.: Prentice-Hall, Inc., 1967), p. 13.
[3] Ibid.
[4] David W. Miller and Martin K. Starr, *op. cit.*, p. 14.

it. But, wait a minute! What do we know about the process of deciding?

From experience, we know a great deal about the results of business decisions, how Ford's Edsel flopped or how the Mustang succeeded. Little, however, is known of the actual decision-making drama that preceded the introduction of these models: the striking of tradeoffs between conflicting goals, the hunches, the uncertainty, anxiety, and tension during the incubation period when management was comparing and evaluating a number of alternatives based on risky assumptions. However, after everything was balanced and weighed, a choice had to be made! But how was it made?

It is vital for the effective manager to understand the issues and answers to a number of questions surrounding the decision-making process:

1. What processes are used in making decisions in business?
2. Is there a specific sequence of steps that should be taken?
3. What is the role of intuition in decision making?
4. How are the tradeoffs made on multiple criteria?
5. Do different managers decide in different ways?

This book, like others in the Winthrop Management Series, is quite unique. It is built around a dialogue which appears at the end of each chapter. The panelists in the dialogue were, in the opinion of the authors, a representative cross section of modern managers and entrepreneurs. Participating in this dialogue were seven panelists, plus the two authors of the book. Perhaps the most unique characteristic of the panel members is that they were all candidates for an MBA degree. The panelists are introduced before the actual dialogue begins at the end of Chapter Two.

WHY A PANEL DISCUSSION?

It is important to understand why we have included the dialogue. First of all, we hope it will lend relevance to many of the ideas presented in the text, as the panelists discuss how some of these ideas apply in their daily lives. Secondly, the panelists develop additional ideas in the course of the dialogue which augment many of the ideas in the text. Thirdly, it is hoped that the dialogue will provide a mechanism for integrating many of the decision-making concepts of this book with ideas covered in other texts in this series. Finally, it is hoped that the panel discussion will do something that textual presentation cannot do—namely, *dramatize* ideas rather than just explain them.

It would be presumptuous for us to predict what impact, if any, this small book will have upon you as a manager. Nevertheless, it is not presumptuous for us to share our hopes with you. We hope that as you read you will discover some insight into the answers to some of the questions we have raised about decision making in business. We hope that this insight will distill into opinions for discussion and argument. Finally, it is our hope that the opinions will give you a good "feel" for how you can improve your own problem-solving and decision-making style both in your personal and professional life.

SUMMARY

The process of *knowing* what to do, or *deciding*, is basic not only for each individual personally, but also for each individual as a professional manager. A manager's main orientation is toward the *making* of decisions, rather than toward the nuts and bolts of carrying out those decisions. There is always an implicit opportunity loss associated with poor decisions. They are the foregone gains, profits, or cost savings, which could have been realized had a better decision been made.

two

Round and Round It Goes, and Where It Stops Nobody Knows

Bruce Meyers

The abandonment of overdrawn distinctions,
particularly dualisms like good-evil,
masculine-feminine, right-wrong, in favor of
a sense of the spectrum of similarities
that underlies experience.

John R. Seeley
Time's Future in Our Time

11

LEARNING OBJECTIVES

When you have completed this chapter you should begin to understand the following:

1. Why business executives often disagree about whether good decision making is an *art* or a *science*.
2. That there are two ways to know things: one is *analytical*, the other is *intuitive*.
3. That it is these two modes of cognition which are the bases for two approaches to decision making.
4. The analytic mode operates by breaking down the whole of a decision into its component parts; the intuitive mode operates synthetically or holistically, grasping the totality of the decision at once.
5. Why it is impossible to make good decisions using only one approach or the other all of the time.

GLOSSARY

Bifunctional Brain The hypothesis that man's brain has two lateral hemispheres with specialized functions. The hypothesis claims that in right-handed people, the left hemisphere tends to specialize in rational knowing while the right hemisphere tends to specialize in cognitive functions usually associated with intuition.

Decisions of Encounter A decision that is encountered resulting from a problem that has arisen suddenly or unexpectedly.

Programmed Decision A decision that arises from a problem which could be anticipated; a planned decision.

Lineal Thinking A term used to describe rational or logical thinking and the inferences consequent upon this type of thinking; also called *analytical, causal,* or *secondary-process* thinking.

Yin and Yang In Chinese philosophy, the yang is the masculine, light, or active principle which combines with the feminine, dark, or passive principle to produce all that comes into being.

How do managers decide things? Is business decision making done mostly on an intuitive basis, or is it done on a step-by-step rational basis? Perrin Stryker in the Introduction to *The Rational Manager* diagnoses the cause of bungled problems and erroneous decisions as irrational and unsystematic thinking by managers.[1] He prescribes the use of a systematic, ic, decision-making process as a panacea for much of the inefficiency and waste resulting from poorly made decisions.

A CONTROVERSY

We were recently involved in a dialogue on the subject of how business executives make decisions. During the dialogue a spirited discussion among participants erupted concerning the merits of trying to construct a general step-by-step process for solving problems and making decisions in management. Is there a series of steps for rational choices that can be implemented in a fairly wide variety of managerial experiences? Or, is each problem situation so unique and filled

[1] Charles H. Kepner and Benjamin B. Tregoe, *The Rational Manager: A Systems Approach to Problem Solving and Decision Making,* (New York: McGraw-Hill Book Co., 1965).

with so many kinks that the manager can do little more than rely on past experience in order to make a decision?

One small group of participants in the seminar maintained that it was impossible to generalize the management decision-making experience. They insisted that the process used to select the best solution is greatly dependent upon environmental and other unique peripheral factors surrounding the problem. As a result, a general model of an ideal system would, of necessity, be so abstract or inflexible that it would probably not reach the threshold of relevance

in the majority of management cases. This group also con-
tended that the most that can be expected of a manager is
that, hopefully, the individual can survive sufficient problem-solving encounters to develop an intuition for making
good decisions more often than bad ones. Another group
of dissidents took an opposite position insisting that decision making, like any process, could be reduced to a specific
series of steps—a kind of "do-it-yourself recipe" for selecting
better solutions to management problems. It was their
belief that this recipe then could be adapted to fit the needs
of a particular management situation. The bulk of the participants in the dialogue appeared to vacillate in their opinions
between the two views defined by the groups, alternatively
agreeing and disagreeing with comments expressed by the
more vocal members of the two groups.

One Theory or Two?

At first it appears that there is a dispute between one
group which insists that a theory of management problem
solving and decision making is impossible, and another
which insists that one is in fact possible. The situation is not
unlike the one depicted in the following vaudeville skit:

> Two comedians stroll on stage. The first comedian says
> in a very annoyed tone, "Theories! Theories! Every-
> body's got a theory! I think all those theories are a
> bunch of bunk, and anybody who invents a theory is
> a fool!"
>
> The second comedian, tongue in cheek, snaps back,
> "I see. Is that *your* theory?"
>
> The first comedian, visibly disturbed, replies, "Yes, as a
> matter of fact, I suppose it is!"

The fact is that both of these diametrically opposed opinions represent two different theories, models, or conceptions of the problem-solving and decision-making processes in management. One theory, however, the *no-theory theory* is more subtle and less explicit in its content than the other.

Is It a Science or an Art?

Whenever there is a lively debate of whether good problem solving and decision making is, or can be, a science, these same two approaches seem to emerge. We shall refer to these diverging paradigms or models of the decision process as *analytical* and *intuitive*. There is a rhetoric of conventional wisdom associated with each paradigm. It is more in vogue these days to be a member of the analytical party. The analytical party champions the cause of what may be called *scientific decision making*. The party rallies around the cry that "pure-hunch decisions are obsolete!" There are a lot of experts in this party called *management scientists* or *decision theorists* who help write the party platform. They are quite explicit about the fact that their platform is based on the theory that good decision making for business problems can be reduced with proper engineering to a systematic selection process. They insist that the goal of decision theory should be to construct an ideal algorithm for rational choice —a broad cookbook procedure, as it were, or step-by-step logical sequence for picking the best alternative as the solution to a management problem. Analytic decision making is also sometimes referred to as lineal or *systematic*. Analytic thinking, the handmaid of rational decision making, is sometimes called logical or *secondary-process* thinking.[2]

There is a second party called the intuitive party. Propo-

[2] Colin Martindale, "What Makes Creative People Different?" *Psychology Today*, July 1975, p. 44.

" FLASH" GORDON, THE INTUITIVE WHIZ KID OF WALL STREET, GETS ANOTHER FLASH AND SAVES THE DAY.

nents of the more conservative intuitive or no-theory party are essentially skeptics whose platform is based upon the belief that good decision making applied to management problems is an art, not a science. The intuitionists hold firmly to the theory that the whole process of knowing the problem and deciding on a solution is largely intuitive and unconscious. They argue that good problem diagnosis and decision making is an esoteric mixture of rare ingredients joined together in some kind of magical fashion, and go under the approximate titles of experience, imagination, intelligence, and feeling. Intuitive decision processes are also referred to as *nonlineal* or *holistic*. Intuitive knowing and understanding, the handmaid of intuitive deciding, is sometimes called *primitive*, *nonrational*, or *primary-process* thinking.

Traces of Schizophrenia

These two distinct positions on the nature of decision processes frequently emerge in discussions. However, an odd thing happens when an attempt is made to neatly divide opinions on the subject into two separate piles: analytical and intuitive. We often end up with two relatively little piles of clear-cut opinions for those whose viewpoints neatly fit into one category or the other, and a huge pile of leftover opinions that apparently do not fit exactly into either of the two original piles. Of course, from one perspective, this is not surprising. We must consider the fact that these two categories of opinion are conceptual extremes which we will seldom encounter in a pure form. However, what is particularly curious is that the opinions in that huge leftover pile manifest a puzzling schizoid tendency to hold both viewpoints simultaneously, just like the third group of participants in the dialogue previously discussed.

After arguing that a step-by-step approach to decision making is desirable, a theorist typically proclaims an ambiguous series of caveats warning that there is no foolproof mechanical procedure for making decisions. To the uninitiated or casual observer, these theorists seem to be somehow contradicting themselves. They seem to be saying, let me show you a systematic procedure for making more effective decisions—and, now that I have shown you this procedure, remember that in the real world, decision making is often quite unsystematic. There are actually far too many peculiarities involved in it for any system to comprehend.

For example in a popular article, "How Businessmen Make Decisions," John McDonald tends to take an analytical position when he comments: "Since the pure-hunch decision is on the way out in business, it is important to understand what is involved in 'rational' decision making."[3] But in other parts of the very same article he reports that most successful decision makers are at a loss to analytically explain how they made the decisions that they did, and that they make their most important decisions subconsciously.[4] In the same article, McDonald also points a distinctly intuitive finger at the fact that after almost ten years of studying business and military "systems" with the aid of the most advanced scientific decision techniques available, Rand Corporation scientists have concluded that no decision mechanism can be devised that will escape the basic uncertainties and complexities that plague large problems of decision.[5]

Charles Kepner and Benjamin Tregoe, well-known management consultants in the field of problem solving and decision making, offer the potential decision maker a systems approach to making decisions. This approach consists of a sequence of what they call "the basic steps which should be followed in any problem-solving and decision-making process." The position assumed by the authors is distinctly analytical. Yet, subsequent to their description of the series of steps involved in their preference model, the authors manifest evidence of the same subtle contradiction when they report that their model will not guarantee successful

---

[3] John McDonald, "How Businessmen Make Decisions," *Fortune*, August 1955, pp. 84–87 and 131–133.
[4] Ibid.
[5] Ibid.

" WELL, HOW DO WE DECIDE, INTUITION OR LOGIC ? "

decision making; that the process is inherently difficult and involves not only experience, knowledge, common sense and judgment, but also a great many future uncertainties that may threaten the action decided upon.[6] It is not difficult to be plagued by the vague feeling that, even if you could

[6] Charles H. Kepner and Benjamin B. Tregoe, *op. cit.*

master their analytical method, you might lack some of the most vital ingredients in knowing what is wrong and what to do about it.

George Odiorne in his popular book, *Management: Decisions by Objectives,* manifests the same type of subtle split in his characterizations of decision making. After presenting his version of a systems model for decision making, also consisting of a number of steps or "stages," Odiorne starts to back off from his lineal position and distinguishes between what he calls the "logic of theory" and the "logic of practice":

> The logic of theory arranges the stages of decision as an orderly, rational process, moving from the setting of objectives to the determination of the final course of action to be taken. It has symmetry, logic and a beginning and an end. The logic of practice is made up by the time and interest of the executive, his pressures, and the day-to-day judgments on numerous decisions which he goes through in a single day. He makes a fragmentary judgment on a single part of a larger problem, then awaits further developments. He seldom has time to stick with one major problem to carry it through two or more stages of action. If the problem has "high priority," he may spend more time on that matter. Usually he must await other's actions, and accordingly, turns his attention to the currently required stage of another of the numerous problems with which he is dealing. The admixture of actions he takes comprises the logic of practice. He is more like a juggler than a weight lifter.[7]

It is hard to avoid being just a little irritated with the conflict inherent in this schizophrenic view of decision making. He appears to be, as it were, indecisive about decision making. It is easy to imagine that what he is really thinking—without

---

[7] George S. Odiorne, *Management Decisions By Objectives,* (Englewood Cliffs, N.J.: Prentice-Hall Inc., 1969), p. 124.

actually saying it—is, something like, even though the model presented in my book is a neat lineal package, in the actual practice, folks, decision making is quite nonlineal!

For the student of decision making this raises some puzzling questions of fundamental importance. Why do these and other writers, who attempt to specify a system or process of deciding in terms of a lineal sequence of logical steps, always seem to terminate their discussions with a defensive apology for some type of vague inadequacy in their model? Why does a certain part of problem solving and decision making always seem to remain fuzzy and ill defined? An appreciation of why this happens is absolutely essential for an understanding of problem solving and decision making in management.

TWO WAYS TO KNOW: ONE STRAIGHT, ONE KINKY

Until a short time ago, it was next to impossible to provide very much insight into many of the questions raised in the last section. As a matter of fact, until recently, we did not even know the proper questions to ask. However, recent conceptual breakthroughs have begun to shed some light on the problem of cognition or knowing. Most of these breakthroughs are hardly recognized as such, for they are occurring mostly in areas of study traditionally relegated to the underworld of managerial psychology. These bits and pieces of insight have yet to be fully elaborated and integrated. They exist for the most part as loose ends of experience that have been formulated into speculations and hypotheses. Their connection with the larger body of psychological theory has not been thoroughly established. Yet the breakthroughs are apparent in the emerging preoccupation of many psychologists with what is becoming known loosely as the *psychology of consciousness.*

We are beginning to admit the possibility that there may be two complementary modes or ways of knowing things. Neither mode may be reducible to the other; and their simultaneous functioning in the same person may be incompatible. One mode of knowing is culturally more familiar and acceptable. Its development is stressed in traditional formal education. It is verbal and rational in orientation, sequential and orderly in operation. It can be characterized by logical or analytical thinking in problem solving and decision making. The other mode of knowing is less familiar to us, at least in Western culture. Its development is stressed more deliberately in the so-called esoteric disciplines of Eastern culture. It is intuitive and holistic in orientation, diffuse and nonlinear in operation.

A Bifunctional Brain

Robert Ornstein, a psychologist and popular writer in this area, relates these two different approaches to knowledge to the concept of the bifunctional brain in man.[8] The cerebral cortex of the brain is divided into two hemispheres joined together by a large bundle of interconnecting nerve fibers. He stresses the point that since the 1860s, neurological evidence has been slowly building on the differential specialization of these two cerebral hemispheres. The left hemisphere of most human brains seem to specialize in the functions of language, rational knowing, a sense of time, and the other linear functions. The right hemisphere, in most instances, appears to favor nonverbal thinking and knowing like intuition, spatial orientation, the direction of many artistic

[8] Robert E. Ornstein, *A Psychology of Consciousness,* (San Francisco: W. H. Freeman and Company, 1972).

activities, and other nonlinear functions. In the words of Ornstein:

> Both the structure and function of these two "half-brains" in some part underlie the two methods of consciousness which simultaneously coexist in each of us. Although each hemisphere shares the potential for many functions, and both sides participate in both activities, in the normal person the two hemispheres tend to specialize. The left hemisphere (connected to the right side of the body) is predominantly involved with analytic, logical thinking, especially in verbal and mathematical functions. Its mode of operation is primarily linear. This hemisphere seems to process information sequentially. This mode of operation of necessity must underlie logical thought, since logic depends upon sequence and order. Language and mathematics, both left-hemisphere activities, also depend predominantly on linear time.
>
> If the left hemisphere is specialized for analysis, the right hemisphere (again, remember, connected to the left side of the body) seems specialized for holistic mentation. Its language ability is quite limited. This hemisphere is primarily responsible for our orientation in space, artistic endeavor, crafts, body image, recognition of faces. It processes information more diffusely than does the left hemisphere, and its responsibilities demand a ready integration of many inputs at once. If the left hemisphere can be termed predominantly analytic and sequential in its operation, then the right hemisphere is more holistic and relational, and more simultaneous in its operation.[9]

The recognition of the idea that we possess two cerebral hemispheres, which probably tend to specialize in different

[9] Robert E. Ornstein, *op. cit.*, pp. 51-53.

modes of knowing, may permit us to understand much more about the fundamental duality reflected in the way we "make sense" out of problems, make "best guesses" about their solutions, and arrive at decisions. It is the combination or integration of these two modes of thinking and knowing that is likely to underlie genuinely creative decision making.

In the business world it is not unusual to observe an engineer or industrial scientist who manifests a distinct preference for a lineal approach in solving problems and making decisions; and, who may forget, downgrade, or even deny the other problem-solving approach. The individual's analytical predisposition is rooted in early training and perpetuated by biases. The person might experience difficulty in communicating and working with people in areas like sales promotion, public relations, and marketing that use different styles of decision making. But these other intuitive styles of decision making, less logical and precise though they may be, are absolutely essential for the solution of some problems and the making of some decisions. This is the root source of much of the conflict and confusion which constantly surfaces in discussions on: Is "good" decision making systematic? The simple fact is: Any attempt to reduce all decision making entirely to a programmed sequence of orderly steps is doomed to failure. It is frankly impossible!

Complements, Not Substitutes

Intuition is not an inferior form of cognition that needs to be superseded by reason and logic. The two modes of knowing and deciding are not substitutes, but complements; two pillars offering separate but equal support to the decision-making and problem-solving process. They are the yin and the yang of knowing and deciding. The impracticability of replacing intuition with analysis is what underlies statements like those of George Odiorne affirming that

part of the decision process remains "imponderable."[10]
The Italian psychiatrist, Roberto Assogioli gives an excellent
description of the articulation of the two distinct ways of
thinking and knowing in controlled mental activities like
problem solving and deciding.

> We will consider intuition mainly in its cognitive func-
> tion, i.e., as a psychic organ or means to apprehend
> reality. It is a synthetic function in the sense that it
> apprehends the totality of a given situation or psychic
> reality. It does not work from part to whole—as the
> analytic mind does—but apprehends totality directly
> in its living existence. . . .
>
> To speak more directly, and without metaphor, of the
> true relation between intuition and intellect, intuition
> is the creative advance toward reality. Intellect (needs
> first, to perform) the valuable and necessary function
> of interpreting, i.e., of translating, verbalizing in ac-
> ceptable mental terms, the results of intuition; second,
> to check its validity; and third, to coordinate and to
> include it into the body of already accepted knowledge.
> These functions are the rightful activity of the intellect,
> without its trying to assume functions which are not in
> its province. A really fine and harmonious interplay be-
> tween the two can work perfectly in a successive rhythm:
> intuitional insight, interpretation, further insight and
> its interpretation, and so on.[11]

Specifically in terms of problem solving, intuition can act
as an efficient data-reduction system ignoring the superficial
symptoms and focusing perception directly on the root causes
of a difficult management problem; analysis can serve a
very useful verifying function. Intuition can be used to gen-

[10] George S. Odiorne, *op. cit.*, p. 119.
[11] Robert Assogioli, *Psychosyntheses*, (New York: The Viking
Press, 1971), pp. 217–224.

erate new alternatives for a strategic decision; logic can be used to systematically screen them.

THE DIFFICULTY WITH AN OVERLY RIGID SYSTEMATIC DECISION MAKING PROCESS

"IF MY ASTROLOGICAL CALCULATIONS ARE CORRECT, YOU WILL SOON BE PLAYING FULLBACK FOR THE NEW YORK JETS."

Another fruitful way of implementing intuition in order to complement systematic decision making is in the process of assessing the relative importance of one decision criteria for a particular decision over another; or, in the process of evaluating different alternatives against several of those criteria when there is insufficient hard data to do it on a sound analytic basis. For example, suppose we are trying to choose which of two elegantly styled sport cars to purchase. For simplicity, let us also assume that these two cars are exactly alike in all respects, but differ only, so far as we know, on the basis of symbolic "status" and "dependability." Finally, let us suppose that the information regarding the importance of these criteria to us that we have accumulated is, at best, vague and ambiguous. Intuition can assess the relative importance or value of status over dependability, or vice versa. It might also be used to rank each car, first on the basis of its dependability, and then on the basis of its symbolic status value.

The complementary working of logic and intuition is hardly new. The incomplete nature of analytic knowledge is described aptly in the old tale of the blind men who were trying to *know* or *understand* what an elephant was.

It seems that some sightless members of a blind community were trying to learn about an elephant. Since none of them had ever seen one before, they decided to gather information by each one touching some part of it. When some other members of the community asked them to describe an elephant, they were told different things:

The man who touched an ear said: "It is a large, rough thing, wide and broad, like a rug."

The man who felt the trunk said: "It is like a straight and hollow pipe."

One who had acquainted himself with its feet and legs said: "It is stiff and firm like a pillar."

Each man had felt one part of many. Each had perceived it wrongly. No one knew all: *Knowledge is not a companion of the blind!*

Logical reasoning is analytical, piecing together the elements in the conceptual puzzle: What is an elephant? The elephant is known in terms of its parts. Intuition supplies a holistic cognitive reinforcement so that the answer to the cognitive puzzle becomes more complete. The elephant is known in another holistic way. The ancient myth of the blind men and the elephant is often used to communicate the fact that it is impossible, or at least foolish, to try to know a thing completely by logical analysis. The consciousness of a need for some type of a synthesis of intellect and intuition in solving problems and making decisions is not restricted to folk tales and parables. Einstein has been quoted as saying, "There is no logical way to the discovery of the elemental (physical) laws.[12] There is only the way of intuition, which is helped by a feeling of order lying behind their appearance."

Examples that suggest the integration of intuition and logic in scientific discovery are numerous. Jacques Hadamard, searching for patterns of creative problem solving in mathematics, suggests that we stop laboring on a problem when no further progress seems possible.[13] Then, return to the original problem after an extended interval of time, perhaps several months, after which the solution will probably be found in a relatively short period of time. Dr. Otto Loewi, a Nobel prize winner in 1936, furnishes an excellent practical example of

[12] Quoted in W. I. B. Beveridge, *The Art of Scientific Investigation*, (New York: Random House, 1957), p. 77.

[13] Jacques Hadamard, *The Psychology of Invention in the Mathematical Field*, (Princeton, N.J.: Princeton University Press, 1945).

successfully following Hadamard's formula in his description of how he demonstrated the chemical theory of the transmission of a nervous impulse. The original hypothesis occurred to him 17 years prior to the time when he suddenly awoke one night and realized that he had discovered a simple experiment that could finally test his original hunch.

It All Depends

If a manager is working on decisions involving a substantial degree of repetition, an orderly sequence of steps for deciding which solution is best is probably appropriate. In addition, it helps if the decision can be anticipated and does not involve significant ambiguity either in the decision criteria or in the data supporting the decision. In decisions of this type, which are sometimes referred to as **programmed decisions**, the role of intuition is probably below the threshold of relevance much of the time.

There are other factors that tend to reduce the need for intuition; and, correspondingly, tend to enhance the value of a systematic approach involving significant analysis and computation. If some of the following conditions are a part of the decision-making context, an analytic approach to the decision process is probably more relevant:

1. There is enough lead time and budget to afford data gathering and analysis.
2. There is an adequate quantity of *hard* as opposed to *soft* data. That is, some of the data should warrant being quantified.
3. The environment of the decision must be reasonably stable. That is, everything surrounding the decision cannot be changing so fast that the decision maker cannot even name which outcomes of the decision

are relevant. If the environment is this unstable, and he cannot insulate his decision from its impact, he must learn to fly by the seat of his pants.

4. The decision maker must also either possess the skill himself, or have access to resources that do have the skills, to take an ill-defined decision situation, and translate it into a well-defined research problem with operational concepts so that some of the important relationships can be represented quantitatively.

As a matter of terminology, unforeseeable decisions are sometimes called **decisions of encounter**. Other things being equal, decisions of encounter favor the use of intuition over analysis. Decisions with hard data are sometimes called *objective decisions*. These favor analysis. Decisions with intangible or soft data are sometimes called *subjective decisions*.

With regard to a specific decision, the question is not whether the decision process *can* be broken down into a formula-like series of steps, but whether and to what degree the decision process can be *fruitfully* broken down into a formula-like series of steps. This will be contingent on a number of environmental factors surrounding the decision. If we are careful to keep in mind the importance intuition might play during each phase, we probably decrease the danger of overlinealizing the decision. If the decision can be linealized into a series of steps without sacrificing the cross fertilization between logic and intuition, the linealization will facilitate rather than hinder effectiveness.

We hope that this chapter has not inadvertently led to the conclusion that problem solving and decision making in management are either inherently intuitive or analytical. We do not advocate junking logical analysis either as a recommendation or as an innuendo. Carried to extremes, such an approach is at least fatuous and probably suicidal. Quite the contrary is true. A *system* for decision making is not wrong per se: the real trouble is that it is frequently misunderstood. It is not that the concept of decision making as a logical process is not useful; it is often misused. It must be clearly understood that good problem solving and decision making involve some kind of personally palatable synthesis of the two complementary approaches to knowing a problem and its solution: the rational and the intuitive. If this is understood, then a systematic approach to problem solving and decision making will facilitate rather than frustrate the union of logic and intuition. A system can assist in giving the necessary focus to intuition for making the appropriate comparisons.

What we are seeking is a rational framework for decision making, not a process consisting of programmed sequence of rigid steps.

SUMMARY

Whenever there is a spirited debate over the problem of whether good decision making in business is a science or an art, two fairly distinct views or opinions seem to emerge: a lineal view which champions a scientific or analytical approach, and a nonlineal view which favors an intuitive approach. Many writers on management decision making manifest a puzzling and ambiguous schizoid tendency to hold both extremes of opinion simultaneously.

We are learning that there are two complementary ways of knowing things: one is analytical, the other is intuitive. It is this duality in the way we know things that is frequently being reflected in the two approaches to decision making. An appropriate integration of these two modes is likely to underlie genuinely creative decision making.

We do not advocate junking either logic or intuition. What we are seeking is a rational framework for decisions, not anything even approaching a programmed sequence of rigid steps—something rational and *beyond*.

SKILL DEVELOPERS

1. Discuss what conditions usually surround a decision exist when deciding the "best" thing to do, must be largely intuitive. Suggest some examples.
2. Why is it said that pure-hunch decision making is on its way out in business? Is it true?
3. Getting so close to a problem that "you can't see the forest for the trees" is an example of overlinealizing a problem. In decision making it can lead to *analysis paralysis*. Discuss this statement and relate it to the tale of the elephant and the blind men.
4. Discuss what is meant by the vague statement that intuitive knowing works in a nonlineal, simultaneous manner. Suggest an example.
5. Discuss the distinction between *programmed decisions* and *decisions of encounter*. Suggest examples.
6. Discuss the meaning of the statement, "knowledge is not a companion to the blind," in the tale of the elephant and the blind men. Blind to what?
7. What is meant by the statement, "intuition suggests and logic validates?" Explain.
8. Speculate on why business executives might be reluctant to admit that much of their decision making is intuitive.
9. Intuition is sometimes referred to as "knowing without thinking." This statement appears somewhat contradictory. Explain.
10. Discuss briefly why intuition is called a *nonlineal process*.

PANEL DISCUSSION

The participants in the dialogue are introduced in the order in which they enter the conversation. A brief biographical sketch on each panelist has been included.

Edward (Ed) Sanford is a co-author of the text. He is a Professor of Management in the quantitative methods area at Pepperdine University's School of Business and Management. He is a consulting economist and statistician, specializing as an expert witness in legal cases involving damage measurement resulting from alleged antitrust or tort violations.

Robert (Bob) Wade has been employed by a number of the largest advertising agencies in the country including J. Walter Thompson Company, an N. W. Ayer affiliate, and Erwin Wasey Advertising. He has been a copywriter, creative supervisor, and Vice President. Today he works as a freelance copywriter specializing in brochures, direct-mail literature, and campaigns for clients throughout Southern California. He also owns and operates "The Brass Forest Antiques," a retail store in Studio City, California.

Harvey Adelman is a co-author of the text. He is also a Professor of Management in the quantitative methods area at Pepperdine University's School of Business and Management. He is a consulting psychologist and statistician, specializing in sample survey research and measurement theory.

William (Bill) Fisher is a sales support engineer with Xerox Corporation. He is a manufacturer's representative for the analysis and solution of software problems in a computer-centered system. With a B.S. in Industrial Engineering, Bill has a broad background in engineering, communications, and electronics. He has specialized in the computer fields of system design, programming; debugging and checkout, technical editing of program documentation, and the training and supervision of programmers and program analysts.

Leonard (Len) Slaughter, Jr. is a Senior Consultant for the Los Angeles based Institute for Economic Research. He has specialized in the areas of urban planning and economic development. He is also involved in the areas of human resource and social service planning. Before becoming a consultant, Len was a former District Supervisor for the Community Action Division, a Chief of the Housing Branch of the Office of Program Development, and finally, a Director of the Community Development Division for the Office of Economic Opportunity in Washington, D.C. Len is also a former Princeton Fellow in Public Affairs.

Annette Kelleher has been an associate director of the Space Test Program of the Aerospace Corporation in El Segundo, California. The Space Test Program launches two to four satellites each year. Annette is currently involved in corporate strategic planning, new business development, and marketing. She has also been a staff engineer in the Information Processing Division, and a Manager of Flight Operations on the Manned Orbital Laboratory at Aerospace Corporation. She has been a consulting design and control systems analyst with the Autonetics Division and the Missile Division of North American Aviation, and Robert-Shaw-Fulton Controls. She has also acted as a consultant in piping and vessel stress analysis with M. W. Kellogg Company, Ralph M. Parsons, Inc. Inc., and the Bechtel Corporation.

Harold (Hal) Solomon migrated to California from Pennsylvania in 1961 where he joined Douglas Aircraft as a scientific programmer/analyst. He was employed by Computer Sciences Corporation to work on the development of a real-time telemetry data reduction system for the Mariner and Surveyor Space flights. He has been a group leader at Aerospace Corporation involved with the development of computer programs for the reduction and analysis of data from launch vehicles and orbiting satellites. When he was with the Measurement Analysis Corporation he was involved in the development and marketing of proprietary software packages. He has been with the Advanced Information Systems Group of McDonnell Douglas Astronautics where he performs systems analysis for the engineering laboratories and advanced projects group. He is now an Area Manager in the Engineering Computing Department of Hughes Aircraft Corporation at their Canoga Park and Malibu facilities.

Kenneth (Ken) Brown is a Senior Manufacturing Engineer with Xerox Corporation. He has been a supervisor of Manufacturing Engineering with Electronic Memories Corporation, a supervisor of Industrial Engineering with I.T.T. Aerospace, a production superintendent with Canoga Electronics Corporation, an Industrial Engineer with the Bendix Corporation, and a Manufacturing Planner with Litton Systems. He specializes in production management, planning, design and tooling, as well as capital equipment planning and budgeting.

Richard (Rich) Collato is an executive director of the San Pedro and Peninsula Y.M.C.A. in Southern California. He has also served as executive director of the Huntington Beach-Foundation Valley Branch of the West Orange County Y.M.C.A. also located in the Los Angeles area. He has also served as director of health and physical education for the Highland Park Branch of the Greater New York Y.M.C.A. Rich is a skilled management consultant and has directed his own insurance brokerage firm. He has developed a Y.M.C.A. surfing program, written a Y.M.C.A. surfing manual, and a teaching manual for instructors.

The dialogue took place at Pepperdine University's Center for International Business in the World Trade Center in downtown Los Angeles, California, at 6:00 p.m. in the evening on July 2, 1975.

Ed: Our general topic is problem solving and decision making in business and management. I would like to suggest that we, the participants in this panel, initially address the topic of "How we experience problem solving and how decision making is actually being done." What are the relevant processes that the members of this panel have actually observed? I know the members of this panel come from a variety of business backgrounds. Some of you are involved in basically entrepreneurial endeavors; others are from corporate line or staff positions.

Bob: I really can't answer how I make decisions, but I think I can answer why, or at least when, I make them. Bottom line, it comes down to time pressure. I wait and make decisions when I sense that the time is right. What I mean by that is, I wait until time dictates that I have to make it now!

Ed: Bob, would you please explain more fully what you do when you experience pressure to make a decision?

Bob: On every occasion, I try to keep my final decision unresolved and open until the last minute. I might change my mind many times considering numerous possibilities before I make a final decision. On the other hand, sometimes I won't change my mind at all. One of the key factors in this process is being able to sense when the situation dictates, "Now's the time!" To me this is a crucial element in the decision-making process.

Harvey: Do you classify *not making a decision* a form of decision?

Bob: No, not exactly. I classify *not making a decision* as simply keeping all my options open until the situation dictates making the decision.

Ed: Why do you think that you do that?

Bob: I guess I do that because I like to keep getting as much relevant input and letting it simmer on the back burner as long as possible before I make my final choice.

Bill: Yes, I seem to agree with Bob. I find that sometimes if I wait either more data emerges or something happens so that the decision gets made for me. That's a relief, particularly if it's one of those hairy decisions. Let's say I'm supposed to decide something by a 3:30 p.m. deadline. At 3:00 p.m., something happens. It's out of my hands. Some external factor comes to bear that makes the decision for me. I breathe a sigh of relief. I'm glad then I didn't decide the issue at 1:00 p.m., before the external factor came to bear. Maybe it's deserting my responsibility. Maybe it's waiting for more information, I'm not sure. I guess I've never been that introspective about it. But anyway, I agree with Bob, at least on the hairy decisions, I try to wait as long as possible.

Ed: I hear you saying that you won't decide until you know that a further postponement of the decision will result in a loss.

Bill: Yes, I'll keep it cooking on the back burner as long as I still feel comfortable.

Ed: This ability of the decision maker to foresee or postpone a decision is related to the distinction that is sometimes drawn between *programmed decisions* and *decisions of encounter*.[14] But, tell me, what type of risk level have we been talking about in decisions; decisions involving high risk or decisions involving low risk?

Bob: Well, I've been talking about either type of decision, high-risk decisions and low-risk decisions. I think I can break the decisions I make into those two categories. In the case of high-risk decisions, I could be risking my money, my reputation, my self-esteem or anything of significant value that I fear losing. I can't think of any decisions that somehow can't be put into one of these two categories.

[14] C. W. Taylor and F. Barrow, *Scientific Creativity*, (New York: Wiley, 1963).

Len: I would like to make a comment relating Bob's idea of risky decisions to the subject of a relevant temporal framework, or time constraint. It's important for me to know how long I have before I must make the decision. In a risky decision situation I need as much time as possible to plan and investigate the consequences of each alternative. The longer I've got, the more I can plan, gather additional information, hunt for new alternatives, and so forth. In other words, what probably happens is that when I have a lot of time I experience more control of the decision-making process. I make what Ed has called a programmed decision. If this is the case, I become more patient and lineal; that is, I use some fairly systematic or logical process to investigate cause and effect relationships. In general, I become analytical only if I have the time. When time is of the essence, that is, if I face what Ed has called a decision of encounter, irrespective of risk, I tend to rely more on an intuitive approach. I've learned to trust my intuition.

Ed: How did you learn to trust your intuition, Len?

Len: (Laugh) By using it. It's proved out. When I've used it, it's worked. And when I have had the requisite intuition and haven't used it, things have invariably fouled up. When I have been conscious of having it and haven't followed it, things have gone wrong!

Annette: You have some kind of track record of successes. Is that what you are saying?

Len: That's right.

Harvey: Is a success to you, Len, when the outcome occurs the way you predicted it?

Len: Yes.

Hal: I see two aspects to this subject we're talking about.

The first is the decision-making aspect; the second is the problem of conveying that decision to others. At Hughes Aircraft where I'm employed, I'm often involved in risky decisions to make large capital outlays for computing systems. I often rely on my intuition to make the final decision. An example of what I am talking about occurred in the last several weeks. I felt that my director favored a certain type of computer. I took a long period of time to thoroughly investigate the advantages and disadvantages of the computer he suggested, because I had a feeling it was not the proper way to go. I chose another computer. Today just prior to my presentation, some additional input came to light from the Office of the Controller and Division Manager. Everyone that I talked with agreed that I had made the right decision in choosing the hardware that I did despite the fact that it cost more money. Intuitively I always felt it was a better selection. I would like to add that I felt it was right long before the input from the controller's office helped me to justify it analytically. Even though my approach appeared analytical, it was really used to corroborate my intuitive decision.

Harvey: Are you saying that you have to supply your director with analytic input, that is, reasons that justify your decisions because he does not know, like you know, that you can trust your intuition.

Hal: Yes.

Bill: One thing I've learned in making decisions is that once the decision is made, it's important not to worry about the opportunity costs associated with foregone alternatives. If I'm always concentrating on what I could have gotten, but didn't get, because I made the wrong decision, it's distracting. I think it's important to stay in the here and now, and worry about how to make the most of the decision that was made. So, for example, if one alternative I had was a date with Racquel Welch and another alternative was a date with Ann

Margaret, but instead, I chose to go on a date with my wife, then I feel it's important not to fantasize what could have happened on the other two dates. Stay in the here and now, I want to have the best time ever with my wife.

Len: I find decisions for me have a certain *feeling.* They either feel good or they don't. I know I've made the right decision when it feels just right.

Ed: Len, let me try to clarify something in my own mind. When you say, "it feels just right," when does this intuitive feeling occur? Does it occur right after the decision is made, before it is implemented?

Len: Yes, I think so, but my memory is vague about when it starts—that is, when feeling "good" about the decision starts! I think it occurs when I get a breakthrough on some facet of a problem that I've been wrestling with. I get that feeling. Hey, I'm on it! And it begins to feel good even though I haven't solved it yet. I feel like I'm getting hot! I can feel the motion, and I know I'm moving in the right direction. I feel comfortable about what's happening. It's like shooting a basket in basketball and you turn your back away from the basket even before the ball strikes the backboard: you still know you're going to sink it. You just know that you're on the right track. It comes to me as a feeling!

Ed: What does it feel like?

Len: It feels good.

Ed: That's very interesting. W. J. J. Gordon in his book *Synectics* observed that certain people repeatedly selected ways of thinking about a problem that led to elegant solutions. These people confessed to a pleasurable feeling—a feeling of being on the right track—long before their intuition proved correct.[14a]

[14a] W. J. J. Gordon, *Synectics*, (New York: Collier, 1961), p. 29.

Ken: To me, decisions seem to fall into two categories: subjective and objective. The objective decisions almost make themselves. When I have enough data for an objective decision, it becomes apparent what decision I have to make. It is usually more a problem of data gathering and quantification. The subjective decisions that I make are ones that approach a no-risk situation. That is, either option seems good. These are the ones that give me the greatest problem. My wife and I have been involved in a subjective decision concerning what color we're going to paint our house. We have discussed the matter back and forth through two paint sales, and still haven't painted the house.

Harvey: Ken, is that decision problem occasioned by the nature of the content of the decision, or by virtue of the fact that there are two decision makers?

Ken: I think it's due to an absence of role for me. As a manager, I know what is expected of me. I'm expected to make a decision. When I'm deciding things with my wife, my role is absent.

Harvey: When you're making a decision at the office, trying to please your boss, is that conceptually different from making a decision at home, trying to please your wife?

Ken: I suppose there's a "trying to please" aspect to both situations, but at work I have to sell the decisions that I make to somebody else. I feel better when my boss says, yes!, you made the right decision! I'm looking for positive reinforcement along the way. If I don't get it, and if I don't feel strongly about one alternative or the other, I will look at the facts all over again, and perhaps, I will even rationalize the decision in favor of another alternative.

Ed: I am intrigued by the barrage of comments that have been made concerning the intuitive nature of your decision processes. Does that mean that most of your decisions do not follow any step-by-step process? Are you saying that when you are analytical, it is simply a rationalization of your intuition—a kind of ruse or trick to sell your boss? Is most of your decision making the result of a finger snapping insight?

Annette: As I listen to many of the comments that are being made by this group on this issue, and reflect upon the decisions I have made, I am almost appalled at the rapidity with which I make my decisions. I do most of them intuitively in spite of all my analytical training. But, if I'm in the position of accepting someone else's decision I usually demand some reasons, or what we have called analytical rationale, before I accept his decision.

Ed: Do you mean that you're going to demand some reasons to justify it?

Annette: Indeed, I would. Right now, I am involved in a managerial function where I am asking a subcontractor to make a decision. He is to make the decision, but I want to know, in very specific terms, the analytical basis for it. On the other hand, if I had his job, I would want to say, trust me. I know what's important. I would tend to proceed on my gut feelings.

I see two types of decision processes; and, I suppose that the time available is crucial. This subcontractor of whom I speak is paid well for writing up a neat analytical statement as to why he is making a decision in a certain way. That is his job. He is paid to put together a rationale on the front end, before the decision is made. Whereas when I make my personal decisions, which may be anything from buying a house, to accepting a job transfer from Los Angeles to Washington, D.C., I don't have a lot of time. My decision has to be made fast.

Harvey: Annette, may I ask you a question? If you go to a physician who you are paying, like you are paying your subcontractor, and he tells you that you have neurodermatitis, would you ask him to give you his decision rules for arriving at that decision?

Annette: I would have to say, yes. In fact I can cite a particular example, not with myself but with my daughter, where I had a gut feeling that the doctor's diagnosis was wrong. And he replied with the question, "Do you think that my diagnosis is wrong or my treatment is wrong?" I said, "I think your treatment is standard. I'm sure most of the doctor's use this kind of treatment. Therefore, I believe that your diagnosis must be wrong. I would like your records so that I can have another physician give an opinion." I needed a logical reason for his diagnosis. So the answer is, yes, I would require analytic justification. But in my own personal life, and even in professional decisions involving a great deal of money, I may use a gut, or intuitive feel based on some type of broader experiential wisdom. Now, where the broadly based experiential wisdom comes from, I don't know. It seems to be there when I need it. I guess that's why I get paid more than someone 20 years my junior.

Ed: In other words, what I hear you saying, Annette, bottom line, is that you don't consciously use much of an analytical process. Does anyone here use a step-by-step process for making decisions?

Hal: I think there are two separate issues involved in the problem-solving, decision-making process. The first is the process of coming to the decision; the second is convincing others that that decision is correct. I don't think that you can divorce one from the other. And responding to something that Bob said earlier, time is often an important element in determining just how analytical I will be in making a decision. I use lead time, if it is available, for gathering data that will convince others that my decision is indeed the best. I collect this data, and then I find myself involved in the game of trying to put the data together in such a way that it will convince or persuade others that the decision I made, intuitively, is the right one.

Bill: I was sitting here thinking about what Ken said about the two categories of decisions—the subjective and objective distinction. At the same time I was trying to integrate that comment with a comment Len made about getting the feeling that you know when you make the right decision. Suddenly, I began to relate to an incident that occurred in my own life. After my divorce, I looked for an apartment for six months. I don't know how many dozens of apartments I looked at, even though I knew generally what I was looking for in an apartment. I guess that I must have looked at over 100 apartments. One day when I entered an apartment something felt just right. It just felt right! It wasn't related to the decision to move out of my previous house or separate from my wife. I had already done that six months before. As I hunted for apartments I would enter an apartment, and it would have nice carpets and drapes but it just wouldn't feel right. And then, finally, it did feel right. It was a highly subjective phenomenon. In another instance at work, which is more objective, I was asked by a subordinate how to proceed on a project. We sat down, analyzed the data we had, and it was abundantly clear in five minutes that there was only one way to go. To me it was a purely lineal, rational decision and there was only one way to go. No ambiguity. To me, the second decision felt like a much more objective thing. I don't look at it as intuitive. The subordinate just hadn't analyzed the data the way I had.

Ed: I would like to agree with your pragmatic distinction between subjective and objective decisions. I believe the distinction observed is based on the perception of the decision maker as to how tangible or quantifiable the data for the decision is experienced to be. Let me explain. The last automobile I purchased was selected on a fairly intuitive basis because the reasons I purchased it were very personal. I remember that I concocted some vague homespun analytical justification, but I always felt the justification was more rationalizing than rational. However, the auto I purchased prior to that was bought mainly as economical transportation, and was selected on a fairly well-defined conscious analytical basis. I purchased the later car considering desirable features or criteria like gas economy, ease of maintenance, and so forth.

Len: Most of the big decisions that I make do follow some type of structured process. That process usually also has a significant amount of analytical elements present in it. But that's because all my decisions affect other people in my environment. Some of those people who are affected are superiors to whom I must justify my decision, especially in professional situations.

The difficulty that I experience is that a step-by-step lineal process doesn't always give me an answer. I run into stone walls, and all of a sudden I realize that the data that I have isn't enough. And that's when intuition proves an effective means of jumping over that hurdle.

Ed: Len, I hear you saying that when the data you have does not provide a clear-cut answer you fall back on intuition. I find that interesting. Not very long ago I was discussing a speculative hypothesis with a couple of colleagues. We hypothesized in a rather informal manner that man—both phylogenetically and ontogenetically—probably evolved instinct and intuition, prior to the development of reason and analysis; that is, primitive man and children probably feel they are right before they analytically know why. I am reminded of a comment by Colin Martindale, a research psychologist at the University of Maine, in an article entitled, "What Makes Creative People Different?", which appeared in the July 1975 issue of *Psychology Today*. He describes what he calls "two types of thinking processes": primitive or "primary-process" thinking, and rational or "secondary-process" thinking.[15] "Primary process" thinking according to Martindale, and I quote, "belongs to the chaotic realm of dreams and reveries, free associations and fantasies, drug highs and mystical trances."[16] It is primary because it seems to precede analytic mental development and because it is associated with the unconscious. Secondary process thinking is logical and rational.

Now, Martindale measured the degree of cortical brain arousal using electroencephalograms (EEGs) to characterize brain-wave patterns. He found that when we are subjectively alert, attentive and analytical, as we seem to be during rational decision making, that the cerebral cortex of the brain evidenced a medium level of arousal. At other times, when brain-wave frequency is low and we are in a relaxed state of reverie or when brain-wave frequency is high and we are in a state of excitement—those times when people have observed the intrusion of intuition—he observed that primary process thought emerges. He concluded that, and I quote again, "from dream states at one end (of the cortical arousal spectrum)[17] to emotional highs at the other; the irrational stuff of new ideas floats in unplanned on a load of brain waves too high or too low to calculate with." Our rational processes seem to function only at medium levels of cortical stimulation."[18]

If I can indulge my preoccupation with this hypothesis a little more, and chase out some obvious implications, we might conclude that what Len may be characterizing in his description of how he "falls back" on intuition when logic fails is a procedure of shifting from "secondary-process" thinking to "primary process" thinking.[19] Of course, it is

[15] Colin Martindale, *loc. cit.*, p. 44.
[16] Ibid.
[17] The parenthesis and the parenthetical comment have been added by the authors for clarity.
[18] Colin Martindale, *loc. cit.*, p. 44.
[19] Ibid.

only speculation, but this may be a kind of subtle mani-
festation of an instinct for survival under stress—the regression to primary thought. When you have to make a decision,
and you haven't got enough information to indicate for
sure what to do, you fall back on intuition and do what you
feel you should! The psychologist Ernst Kris, incidentally,
explains creativity, which probably involves intuition, as
"regression in the service of the ego."[20]

What particularly fascinates me, panelists, is the fact that I
guess I am hearing from you that you are not very far removed from that "primitive" response in making decisions.
Perhaps we experience ourselves as closer to survival more
of the time than we care to admit.

Annette: You know, while I was driving here this evening, I
was reflecting on problem solving as a management phenomenon that I experience. I thought to myself that man's brain
seems to have gotten to a point where he can solve simple
problems with only a few variables very analytically. We can
tally the pros against the cons, and if there are only a few
alternatives, the one that scores the highest provides us with
a clear-cut analytical decision. But I believe many of the
decisions we normally face in business and management are
of an even higher level of complication involving infinitely
more subtleties. A decision may not allow the cost and
time of elaborate computer modeling. It may also involve
many human factors that do not neatly lend themselves
to modeling. In these situations we tend to fall back on
intuition. I have just made a decision to move my place of
employ, and my residence from Los Angeles, California, to
Washington, D.C. This was an enormously complicated decision for me to make. There seemed to be a huge number of
relevant factors, and each one seemed to consist of an endless
chain of interrelated implications. Now, maybe these could
indeed be quantified and put into a mathematical model on

[20] Ibid.

a computer. However, I think that in this latter type of problem where we have a very sophisticated level of complication, we don't have any effective analytical process that will provide adequate examination of data. I'm not even sure we have that much in the way of hard data. The only effective process seems to be intuitive. At least at my I.Q., the best I can do with this type of problem is throw it back there somewhere. Let it settle, and sift, until I can come up with some type of gut feeling about the right way to go. This initial gut feeling is usually reinforced by subsequent insight which seems to develop as time goes on until I reach my final decision. In any event, whatever happens, usually happens unconsciously. I am beginning to think that I can consciously and rationally handle only simple problems, and the more difficult subtle problems, can only be handled unconsciously.

Harvey: Annette, I wonder if the difficulty that you experience is not an inability to lay out the alternatives. If you could lay out the alternatives, then does it not follow that you could rationally weigh each alternative in some systematic manner and reach a fairly clear-cut decision?

Annette: I'm not so sure that that could ever be done, because the way I experience this problem is that the alternatives involved in my decision imply further alternatives, each one requiring another decision. It's an extremely complex chain of causality. The decision tree of alternative outcomes seems to expand beyond comprehension very quickly. But somehow there's something that happens unconsciously in my brain where I can intuitively say, "Aha! this one is 'right!' I will move to Washington, D.C."

Ed: I would like to relate to something that Len said earlier. If I am making a decision in a managerial context, and I am unable to define a payoff or criterion function because of ambiguity or vagueness, I will invariably fall back on some type of intuitive process. At some point I experience what I think Len made reference to—a flash of insight, surging up from my unconscious, a sudden finger-snapping awareness that emerges almost audibly from my lips as something like, "Oh! I see! Now, I see how the whole puzzle fits together." This is what Hudson Hoagland calls the "Aha! phenomenon."[21] I experience this physiologically happening as a subtle release from stress or tension. What Gordon refers to as a "pleasurable feeling."[22] This initial flash of intuition is, as a rule, subsequently reinforced by further information which emerges or is collected at a later time. The intuition comes first, and this somehow allows me to converge subsequently on an analytical solution.

Annette: I agree.

Len: But that's what I mean. I think the key to the whole situation is somehow related to the amount of time you have to make the decision. If you can take the time to trace out all the alternatives, you might be able to do deliberately what we do by default intuitively. Intuition is just a shortcut when you have no time.

Annette: I think I agree with Len. When we decide intuitively, we're going through some kind of unconscious process of weighing various alternatives very rapidly. In other words, what's happening inside my brain is a very rapid kind of analytic process with the volume turned way down so that I'm not aware of it until I reach a conclusion.

Len: I'm not sure that's genuine intuition. Intuition may be something different. I think we sometimes call that process intuition, but I believe "genuine" intuition is something different. I believe what Annette is referring to is subliminal skill—not intuition.

[21] Hudson Hoagland, "The A-ha! Phenomenon," *Hour of Insight*, Robert M. MacIver, ed. (New York: Books for Libraries Press, 1954, p. 1.
[22] W. J. J. Gordon, *loc. cit.* p. 29.

three

Please Read the Inside of Your Environment Carefully, Before Proceeding

However, all environments are not of the same size, shape, or composition.

E. Frank Harrison,
The Managerial Decision Process

LEARNING OBJECTIVES

When you have completed this chapter you should begin to understand the following:

1. How one decision can be rated as better than another insofar as it achieves the decision maker's objectives to a greater degree.
2. How systematic or rational decision making breaks a decision down into component parts that can be easily tackled.
3. That the power behind systematic decision making derives from the process of taking important considerations from the decision maker's head, externalizing them, and subjecting them to intense scrutiny.
4. Decisions can be classified according to the environment in which the decision is made.
5. Decision-making environments differ concerning outcomes and their probabilities of occurrence.

GLOSSARY

Decision Theory In its broadest sense, any systematic decision process that enables the decision maker to select a best alternative by choosing one that maximizes what is called a utility, payoff, or criterion function. For example, suppose a wholesaler buys widgets for $1 and sells them to retailers for $2 each. The same wholesaler is able to buy gadgets for $1 and sell them for $3 each. Assuming that widgets and gadgets are perfect substitutes so that our hypothetical wholesaler can sell the same quantity of each, decision theory, and common sense for that matter, demand that he sell gadgets if his goal is to maximize profit. In this case a decision theorist would call profit the wholesaler's utility or payoff function. Incidently, note that he incurs a $1 opportunity loss for each widget that he decides to sell.

Environment This is a technical term used to describe the nature of the situation surrounding a decision. More specifically, the term refers to the degree of certainty with which a particular outcome can be predicted if a particular alternative is selected. This degree of certainty might increase either because the decision maker has sufficient information to yield accurate forecasts, or because the individual can manipulate the out-comes.

The use of a rational framework for decision making is called **decision theory**. Decision theory has occasionally been applied as an analytical tool in management for some time. It has been particularly useful in resolving the difficulties inherent in clearly defining what the decision maker means by the best decision possible. This pragmatic term *best* is usually quite subjective. An operational definition of it depends upon the various possible outcomes as well as whatever vaguely defined goals or criteria underlie the decision.

Suppose decision maker A decides to install a computer system to reduce the amount of time required for the preparation of reports. Is the new method better than that currently in use? This question seems almost trivial. We could simply measure and compare the amount of time required for a report with the new system, and then with the old system, to arrive at a satisfactory determination of which is better. However, what if the new system costs $100 per report and the old one costs only $10. Is the possible decrease in time worth the increased price? This is a question of tradeoff between criteria and the relative weight these criteria or attributes bear on the decision. Further, has the new system displaced loyal and trusted workers? Will the satisfaction of the employees decrease with the installation of the computer? These particular criteria for the installation of the computer must be compared and evaluated against the other criteria. They can, therefore, be thought about prior to the decision as an aid in the choice; and after the decision, in order to evaluate the results.

Without a systematic approach the manager might have to lean far more heavily on pure intuition than is appropriate to the situation. The general idea of an analytical approach is to break a potential decision problem into component parts such as:

1. Alternatives.
2. Outcome attributes, or consequences.
3. Objectives.
4. Measurements.

These component parts can be tackled separately and then put back together. In so doing, the relationship of the information to the final decision must be clear. It does not eliminate the manager's use of intuition and judgment. It only focuses it and narrows its scope.

One might well ask wherein lies the power of breaking decisions into pieces for later aggregation. The answer is simply this. We are in a sense taking important considerations from the decision maker's head and subjecting them to intense and systematic scrutiny. The formal steps will be described in some detail later.

DECISION-MAKING ENVIRONMENTS

Decisions are made with varying amounts of information. In general, a lot of credible information is more characteristic of a static rather than a kinetic environmental texture.

The literature in the field of decision theory classifies decisions into the following categories based on environmental conditions.

CHANGING THE ENVIRONMENT FROM RISK TO UNCERTAINTY

"WE'VE DECIDED TO MAKE IT A _TWENTY_ FOOT JUMP INSTEAD!"

Certainty

The choice of a particular decision always results in the same known outcome. For example, suppose the decision maker knows for *certain* that if he decides to price his product at $10 per unit, he will realize $1,000 in sales revenue because at that price the market will buy 100 units. Under such conditions the number of units sold (the outcome) is determined exactly once the price is decided.

Risk

A decision under risk is one in which each action may result in more than one outcome, with each outcome having a known frequency of occurrence based upon theoretical considerations or prior history. For example, betting on number 6 on a single throw of a die has a $\frac{1}{6}$ probability of being correct, based on the fact that there is one way out of six in getting a 6. Or a doctor prescribing Tetracycline may know that there is a 10 percent chance of an anaphylactic reaction, a 75 percent chance of complete remission, and a 15 percent chance of no effect, based on extensive medical records. Most of the traditional work in decision theory in management is of this type.

Uncertainty

A decision may result in many different outcomes and the probabilities of occurrence are not known. In this case neither theory nor existing information give clues about the likelihood of occurrence. For example, a president will not necessarily know who will be the best of three candidates for the office of vice president and therefore does not know which one to promote.

The three types of decisions vary in that the environment of the decision maker differs concerning the outcomes and the probabilities of their occurrence. In the environment of certainty there is only one outcome and it is assumed to occur with a probability of one. In the risky environment there are several outcomes, but we know the percentage of time each will happen. In uncertainty there are several outcomes and we have vague notions about the likelihood of occurrence of each. Most certainty decisions are trivial. The risk decisions are perhaps easy to make because of the mathematical possibilities of determining the outcomes. The uncertainty decisions, which we face most frequently, have the greatest chance of involving intuition. It is an analytical approach to the latter type of decision with which we will be concerned in the next chapter.

SUMMARY

The use of an analytical framework for decision making is called *applied-decision theory*. The heart of the rational approach of applied-decision theory is to break the decision problem into component parts. Decision theory also breaks decisions down into three types depending on the environmental conditions: certainty, risk, and uncertainty.

SKILL DEVELOPERS

1. Identify, to the best of your knowledge, whether the following decisions are made in an environment of certainty, risk, or uncertainty. Give your reasons.
   a. Whether to bet $5 in a crap game in Las Vegas.

    b. Whether to increase your production capacity when you know for sure your sales will increase 5 percent next year.

    c. Whether to go into business with your father-in-law.

    d. Whether to impose additional smog devices on your automobile.

    e. Whether to undergo an open-heart surgery.

2. You are faced with a decision as to whether to introduce toasters or hairdryers as new alternative products to your product line. Develop statements of objectives, attributes, and potential measurements for the decision.

PANEL DISCUSSION

Ed: I would like to briefly discuss how certain characteristics of the decision maker's environment are perceived by this panel to influence the way he makes his decisions.

Rich: I know one important environmental characteristic that influences the way that I make decisions. The way I make decisions depends in part on the amount of power I have to enforce the outcome I want.

Len: Rich, that sounds a little like you're saying that if you make a decision based on an anticipated result that you deem preferable and you have the power to bring about that result —make it happen, then it's the right decision. If you cannot bring about that result by force, then it's the wrong decision.

Rich: I'm just telling you what works for me.

Ed: What I find interesting, Rich, is your response to an uncertain environment. You don't have to be a very good forecaster of the outcomes or results of your uncertain decisions if you always have enough power to ensure that you can bring about those results.

Harvey: In my experience there are three types of decision-making environments: some are filled with uncertainty, others are risk environments where although I don't know what's going to happen I do know the percentage of time it will happen on the average. The third environment is such that I can always either predict or control the outcome and that's what I call decision making under certainty. Rich, maybe your decisions always occur in an environment of man-made certainty because you can control, or to use your vernacular, enforce the outcome.

Ed: What I heard Rich propound was his decision strategy for converting decision making under uncertainty into decision making under certainty. He simply tends to choose alternatives whose outcome he feels he has the power to enforce. In other words, he selects *enforceable alternatives*.

Annette: However, Rich's approach has limited application. If I felt I ought to buy stock, and that this is the right time, I cannot randomly let my pencil drop on the New York Stock Exchange list and select a portfolio, and then take the steps necessary to ensure it is a winner. I would have to gather some type of data on the stocks that I feel would probably make the most money for me. I cannot control the future of those stocks. I cannot simply pick an arbitrary portfolio and then make certain that it will go up in value. I don't have the power to do that. So I would surmise that his strategy would be highly dependent on some other features of the particular environment in which he is making his decision.

Rich: Once again, I'm just telling you what works for me in my environment. Over the long haul I've been very successful, that is, I see myself as having made more right decisions than wrong ones. That's what it's all about in business.

Len: Rich, how do you deal with the situation where you don't have the power to enforce the outcome?

Rich: It's really hard for me to answer that question in the general case.

Harvey: I'm interested in the last statement that Rich made. You're coming from a point, Rich, I take it, where by your own admission you make far more right decisions than wrong ones. So you are satisfied with your ability to make good decisions. Now let's take a hypothetical case of the manager, who probably isn't in management any longer, who has made 90 percent wrong decisions and only 10 percent right ones. Don't you think that he has suffered a serious erosion in self-confidence. How does he go about improving his self-esteem? Can he fruitfully use some analytical system for improving his batting average?

Rich: Yes. I feel like he will no longer be in a position to effectively use his intuitive skills to make good decisions. He's lost his self-confidence. A good analytical system might assist in helping him regain it. I feel it is absolutely necessary to develop self-confidence to be effective over the long haul. Go back to the basketball example; if you're making a lot of baskets and scoring, you've shot a lot. If they're bouncing off the rim, you won't shoot as much, at least not until you ask the coach to check what's wrong with the process that you're using.

Len: I would like to add that although a certain amount of success gives self-confidence, it doesn't necessarily guarantee continued success.

Bob: I think this notion of making right decisions has become even more critical nowadays, especially in the uncertain and unstable environment of big business today. In the past, many organizations survived, even flourished, with executives making 50 percent right decisions during boom times. In fact, that might have been considered a good average for some industries. But times have changed. We live in a much more unstable environment. Things change at an overwhelming pace in a world that feels much smaller. Big business is leveraged to the point that there is a much higher probability that small shifts in demand may make it impossible to absorb enormous fixed costs. We live in a world of scarcity, inflation, foreign competition, adverse public opinion. There are so many potentially threatening factors that have to be weighed and traded off. Once a strategic corporate decision is made and implemented, it may take months and even years to reverse it. This type of environment has forced more reliance on sophisticated planning. Today's business decision maker, in my opinion, must use all of the tools at his disposal. The day of so-called hip-shooting decisions is gone—finis! There's too much at stake. With these kinds of things in mind, I feel certain that analytical decision-making processes will be emphasized in objective decision-making situations. I seriously doubt that intuitive processes will supersede analytical processes. Don't get me wrong! Executives may recognize that intuition is frequently invaluable, but I think that it will tend to be a secretly used thing that they will never openly admit to using. If they do use it, I think that they will rationalize it by trying to dig up data to support it.

four

Getting the Decision Straight

The real trouble with this world
of ours is not that it is an unreasonable world,
nor even that it is a reasonable one.
The commonest kind of trouble is that it is
nearly reasonable, but not quite.

G. K. Chesterton, *Orthodoxy*

LEARNING OBJECTIVES

When you have completed this chapter you should begin to understand the following:

1. How to approach a decision systematically by breaking the process down into eight component steps.
2. How such an articulation of a decision into parts will make decisions more "rational" in the context of the relevant information and criteria.
3. How a systematic decision model can facilitate intuition by focusing it.
4. Why a systematic model will force a decision maker to come to grips with important issues in the decision.
5. How a systematic model can serve as a means by which the rationale for a decision can be communicated clearly to others affected by the decision.

GLOSSARY

Decision Model An analytical method plus the relevant data for making a decision. The relevant information and criteria are the input, and the selected alternative is the output of the model.

Utility A term that is borrowed from economics referring to the satisfaction or benefit associated with something. For example, we might conclude that a left shoe and a right shoe of the same size have more utility to a person than two right shoes of different sizes.

Attribute Scaling The process of developing a one-dimensional measurement scale for assessing the relative utility of each alternative in relation to some attribute. For example, in buying a truck good gas mileage might be considered an attribute. The utility of a particular truck would be measured by its relative gasoline consumption measured in miles per gallon. In other words, the scale used to measure this attribute would be the amount of miles per gallon of gasoline consumed that this truck could get compared to other trucks being considered.

In Chapter Three we identified the essence of the analytical approach fostered by the use of decision theory. We indicated that it is a systematic breakdown of the decision to be made into an articulation of the criteria or attributes for choice. There is probably no one particular analytical method that will serve as an efficient tool for every type of decision. In this chapter we will present a model which offers a good deal of generality and which may, therefore, prove useful in a number of decision-making situations. The model chosen is similar to that used by Newman and Oberstone.[1] The utility of the model, and for that matter any systematic approach, lies in its ability to do two things: (1) put the data into a more useful form; and (2) provide a formula for aggregating the data about each alternative into an overall preference or utility score for those alternatives. The following sections present the framework of a model for use by the manager in making decisions. The steps need not be done in precisely the order given; nor should they all be considered essential for every decision. Nevertheless, they should be viewed as important analytical considerations for the manager in making decisions.

[1] J. Robert Newman and Joelee Oberstone, *Evaluation Technology*, (Unpublished: University of Southern California, 1972).

"IN THE INTERESTS OF SCIENCE, AND DUE TO A LACK OF READILY AVAILABLE ALTERNATIVES, DR. ZOTSKY, I'VE DECIDED TO MAKE WHAT MAY APPEAR AS A RATHER STRANGE REQUEST OF YOU"

A SYSTEMATIC MODEL FOR DECISIONS

Step 1: Problem Definition

First of all a need of some kind must be recognized and articulated. This step may involve a good deal of discovery as well as analysis. The manager must understand and specify the nature of the problem, clearly distinguishing between causes and symptoms. The problem precipitating a decision can often be characterized as a discrepancy between the way things *ought to be* and the way things *are*. A search for the cause of the discrepancy is often a search for the changes that have taken place in the environment that have generated the observed discrepancy.

Step 2: General Goal Statement

Define the goal you are setting out to meet by the decision. This definition should narrow down the focus of general concern. To buy the truck with the largest capacity for hauling, to promote the most effective leader, to realize the largest rate of return on investment all represent examples of the level of generality permissible for this step.

Step 3: Listing of Attributes

The attainment of the goals may require the pursuit of attributes, criteria, or subgoals. These should be listed. In buying the truck, for example, some of the attributes may be "good gas mileage," "low maintenance cost," "high trade-in value," and so forth. As you can see, each of these subgoals is stated as specifically as possible so that actual measurement can be taken later.

Step 4: Development of Constraints

Some of the criteria selected will have implied constraints on them. For example, in the decision to buy a truck the attribute of cost may have an upper limit of perhaps $5,000. A constraint on the promotion of a manager to vice president might be the presence or absence of a technical degree. In any case, any decision alternatives which do not meet these standards or constraints are automatically excluded from consideration.

Step 5: Articulation of Alternatives for Choice

Next, all the possible alternatives for solving the decision problem are listed. Of course, this may involve a good deal more effort in the service of invention and discovery than this statement implies. In the case of purchasing a truck, the choices could be Datsun, Dodge, Toyota, Chevrolet, and others. For promotions, the choices could be among several candidates. These decision alternatives will be the ones to discriminate between by evaluating them with respect to the attributes listed under Step 3.

Step 6: Rank Ordering and Weighting of Criteria

The attributes from Step 3 are then rank ordered in decreasing order of importance. That is, the most important one is listed first, followed by those of lesser importance. Then, assuming that the attributes are not of equal value in determining the final outcome, intuitive weights are assigned to them. The assignment of weights is usually done by subjectively estimating the relative importance of each attribute. For example, in buying a truck we may arbitrarily assign the least important attribute, trade-in value, a value of 10. Then we take the next to lowest, maintenance cost, and assess its value. We could assign a weight of 20 if it were twice as important, 30 if it were three times as important, and so forth. In a like manner we would assess relative weights for each attribute listed. As the list of attributes grows longer, the weights assigned get disproportionately larger; twice as important as 10 is 20, twice as important as 500 is 1,000. Therefore, it is advisable at this point to divide each weight by the total weights (additions of all weights) assigned, and to multiply the result by 100. Thus we have converted the weights into percentages.

Step 7: Develop the Attribute Measures (Utilities)

At this point the decision maker takes each decision alternative and places it on a scale of measurement against each attribute. If the attribute is cost, we can develop a scale which reflects the desirabilities of spending various amounts of money. For example, the Datsun can be placed on the scale, the Dodge, and then the Chevrolet. They should be located on the scale so that the scale number assigned reflects the proper utility benefit or desirability. In the case of truck choices, higher costs would receive a lower utility score. A convenient scale to use is a 100-point scale. By using 100 we can make the assignment of numbers some function of a percentage of the maximum amount we can spend. If a Datsun costs $4,000, then the purchase price of $4,000 could be divided by $5,000, the highest amount we may spend. The Datsun, then, costs four-fifths, or 80 percent of the total amount we can spend. We can, therefore, assign a utility score of 100%–80% = 20% to the Datsun. This same procedure could be used for other attributes as well. Thus, each alternative is scored against each measurement scale for each attribute. Each alternative, then, derives a value or utility for each attribute as a function of its placement or score on the scale.

Step 8: Evaluation of Alternatives

Each alternative has its own measurement which reflects its position or utility score relative to each attribute. Now each of these utility scores is multiplied by the corresponding importance weights assigned to each attribute computed in Step 6. Thus each decision alternative will have a number of utility scores or measures multiplied by the proper weights. These products are called "weighted scores." For each of the alternatives the products, or weighted scores, are totaled. Each of these totals represents the summation of the utilities times weights. The alternative with the highest value is the preferred one for the rational decision choice, other things being equal.

We have just discussed a decision-making system whereby the individual might make a choice among several seemingly equal and desirable courses of action. But wait a minute! What about the case in which the decision maker must take into consideration the viewpoints of others before making a final choice? For example, consider the following:

1. Among the many possibilities of any given space probe, how can the decision maker, say the space probe manufacturer, satisfy the needs of such diverse groups as the scientific community, the various component manufacturers, the military, NASA, and others.

2. How can a decision maker in the criminal justice system decide on the best legislation when the effects are perceived differently by such agencies as the courts, police, attorneys, community leaders, and the like.

In these cases, the interested groups could be empaneled to arrive at the answers to each of the eight steps just discussed. The remainder of the section will outline these procedures as to how they might be applied to a simulated decision; that is, which truck to buy for my corporation.

Let us assume that you are responsible for selecting trucks to service your corporation for the next three years. How would you proceed analytically to select the best fleet?

APPLICATION TO TRUCK-PURCHASING DECISION

Problem Definition

As previously described, the problem is to purchase some trucks to add to your corporate fleet. Involved staff members include purchasing, maintenance, drivers, mechanics, and any other interested corporate personnel. These people become consultants to the decision maker in the form of a panel of experts. In general, they will aid in the structuring of information to be applied later in the selection of alternatives.

Goal Statement

As in most cases, the goal of this decision process is to solve the problem as described. However, something should be added to complete the goal statement. One such statement might be to select the "best make of trucks among all possible choices."

Attributes or Criteria

The panelists or interested parties in the decision could engage in a discussion about the important attributes involved in a *buy decision*. Insofar as possible, the discussion should facilitate the group in reaching a consensus about what is important. Large lists of attributes can be generated. Hopefully, these initial lists can be trimmed into smaller, more pertinent lists of criteria. The final list of attributes should represent a consensus of the panel about the attributes of the decision; that is, information that will aid the decision maker in picking one truck model over the others.

For the purpose of illustration, suppose the group has arrived at five attributes, listed here:

1. *Acceleration Characteristics.* Because of extensive free-way driving the group feels that acceleration to free-way speeds (55 MPH) is important.

2. *Comfort.* Large periods of time spent in driving require comfort considerations.

3. *Maintainability.* Low maintenance costs are always desirable.

4. *Initial Costs.* For most corporations, the monies budgeted for purchases are extremely limited.

5. *Depreciation.* The decline in asset value of a purchase is a viable determinant of the initial acquisition.

These criteria have been selected and a consensus of agreement has been reached. In some combination, these criteria will serve as a guide for the acquisition of pertinent information, and later will be used to make the *buy decision* among the various candidate models of trucks.

Constraints

The next step in the decision process is the development of constraints. Each of the attributes or criteria in the preceding section should be examined for lower or upper limits. For example, the amount of your budget will be a constraint on the initial cost per vehicle. The panel, referred to previously, can also address this question and reach an agreement on this issue. For illustrative purposes, let us assume the following constraints for each of the attributes listed.

Attribute	Constraint
1. Acceleration	0–55 Mph in 14 seconds
2. Comfort	None
3. Maintainability	Less than $1,000/year
4. Initial Costs	Less than $8,000
5. Depreciation	Less than $1,500/year

These constraints represent the limitations on your choices. The models finally selected should at least fulfill the intent of the constraints. If any given model would cost more than $8,000, for example, it would automatically be excluded from further consideration. Therefore, in this step those models that will actually be looked at as possible final choices are selected. In the next step you will consider those candidate models.

Alternative Models

Since you wish to buy trucks, the alternatives to be chosen obviously will be trucks of different makes and models. The panel, in reviewing the previous steps in general and the constraints in particular, have decided that there are four possible candidate alternatives, listed here.

1. Minimax.
2. Maximin.
3. Savage.
4. Hurwicz.

(Actually these trucks are not currently available on the market, but the names protect us from the actual or imagined wrath of real manufacturers.)

There are now four trucks available for selection. Thus your decision of a best or optimal choice has been narrowed to four possible outcomes to which you must apply decision attributes.

Attribute Weighting

For this step, participation should be obtained from the panel members. Perhaps each panelist could rank/order the attributes in their order of importance from 1, the most important, to 5, the least important. One way of doing this is to have each member deliver personal rankings to the decision maker, and then the decision maker can compute averages and report the average ranks. For our illustration suppose you arrived at the following ranks by some form of collaboration or compromise.

Attribute	Rank
Initial Cost	1
Maintainability	2
Acceleration	3
Depreciation	4
Comfort	5

Next, you must weight each of the attributes for its relative importance to the decision. For example, the difference in importance between depreciation and comfort (Ranks 4 and 5) may not be the same as the difference between cost and maintainability (Ranks 1 and 2). Your instructions to the panel of consultants should be, "You have 100 importance points to distribute among the various attributes. These points should be distributed according to how important the attribute is to the decision. If depreciation is twice as important as comfort, it should have twice the number of points. If initial cost is 10 times more important than comfort, it should have 10 times as many points." In other words, we must construct an intuitive scale which attempts to linearize the psychological distance between the importance values of the attributes. The following table provides such a scale.

Attribute	Rank/Order	Weight
Initial Cost	1	40
Maintainability	2	30
Acceleration	3	15
Depreciation	4	10
Comfort	5	5
	Total	100

Since you now have importance weights, and since they total 100, you now have a figure for each attribute that represents its percentage contribution to the overall decisions; that is, which truck to buy. These criteria weights can be thought of as an intuitive assessment of the marginal utility of each attribute for the decision. You also know the information to collect (for each attribute) to help you make your final selection.

DEVELOPMENT OF MEASURES (UTILITIES)

You must now develop a scale for the measurement of each of the five attributes against the four alternatives. These weights will measure the performance of each alternative against each attribute. Here, too, you should typically use a 100-point scale. Treat each attribute separately.

Initial Cost

Most people would hold that within the limits set by the other constraints, the cheaper the truck, the better. Since your cost constraint is $8,000, use that figure as a base line against which to assess the relative burden of cost by each truck. Thus if the Minimax costs $6,000, you would divide the $6,000 by $8,000 and multiply by 100 to obtain 75 percentage points. That number, 75, should then be subtracted from 100 to obtain the scalar measure of performance of 25 points, as follows:

$$100 - \frac{(\$6,000}{(\$8,000} \times 100) = 100 - 75 = 25 \text{ points}$$

Maintainability

Here again you have a dollar figure. Once more, the cheaper the better. Only this time you would use a $1,000 as the denominator to divide into the actual (or predicted) maintenance costs of each vehicle. You would, then, also subtract from 100.

Acceleration

The quicker the acceleration, the better. In this case, 14 seconds is the denominator, and the actual acceleration of each truck is the numerator. The quotient is multiplied by 100, and the product is subtracted from 100 to get the relevant number of points.

" THE REASON YOU CAN'T DECIDE, BUTCH, IS THAT
YOU LACKS THE APPROPRIATE DECISION CRITERIA
AND GOAL STATEMENT. "

Depreciation

Since you have dollars here also, the constraint of $1,500 is used to determine the denominator of the ratio. The historical estimate of depreciation figure is used as the numerator and a rate is determined. The quotient multiplied by 100 is subtracted from 100 to get the performance value in points.

Comfort

For comfort, you must construct a 100-point subjective scale. For this measure, you can provide your panelists with a rating scale for each model and make. One such scale could be: 80–100 is excellent, 60–80 is good, 40–60 is average, 20–40 is fair, and 0–20 is poor. Each of the models could be rated intuitively by each of the panelists, and averages computed. This could represent the comfort index.

EVALUATION OF TRUCKS

Now you should perform the calculations for determining how much of each attribute each truck contains. That is, how much cost, acceleration, comfort and so forth, for each truck currently exists. Assume each truck has the following data associated with each attribute:

Truck	Cost	Maintain- ability	Accelera- tion to 55	Depreciation Per Year	Comfort
MINIMAX	$6,800	900	12 sec	900	90
MAXIMIN	$7,000	700	11 sec	950	60
SAVAGE	$7,500	850	13 sec	850	75
HURWICZ	$7,900	800	10 sec	800	80

These are now converted to the performance scale of 100 according to the following computational scheme:

Truck			Computation									Value

COST

MINIMAX	100	–	(6800/8000	×	100)	=	100	–	85	=	15
MAXIMIN	100	–	(7000/8000	×	100)	=	100	–	88	=	12
SAVAGE	100	–	(7500/8000	×	100)	=	100	–	94	=	06
HURWICZ	100	–	(7900/8000	×	100)	=	100	–	99	=	01

MAINTAINABILITY

MINIMAX	100	–	(900/1000	×	100)	=	100	–	90	=	10
MAXIMIN	100	–	(700/1000	×	100)	=	100	–	70	=	30
SAVAGE	100	–	(850/1000	×	100)	=	100	–	85	=	15
HURWICZ	100	–	(800/1000	×	100)	=	100	–	80	=	20

ACCELERATION

MINIMAX	100	–	(12/14	×	100)	=	100	–	86	=	14
MAXIMIN	100	–	(11/14	×	100)	=	100	–	79	=	21
SAVAGE	100	–	(13/14	×	100)	=	100	–	93	=	07
HURWICZ	100	–	(10/14	×	100)	=	100	–	71	=	29

DEPRECIATION

MINIMAX	100	–	(900/1500	×	100)	=	100	–	60	=	40
MAXIMIN	100	–	(950/1500	×	100)	=	100	–	63	=	37
SAVAGE	100	–	(850/1500	×	100)	=	100	–	57	=	43
HURWICZ	100	–	(800/1500	×	100)	=	100	–	53	=	47

We are now ready to find which truck has the highest value or overall "utility" of each alternative to the decision maker who wishes to use the decision attributes or criteria agreed to in this problem. Each performance value is multiplied by its corresponding utility weight and summed for each model. Thus, the final tabulation is as follows:

	TRUCK			
	MINIMAX Value × WT = T	MAXIMIN Value × WT = T	SAVAGE Value × WT = T	HURWICZ Value × WT = T
Cost	15 × 40 = 600	12 × 40 = 480	06 × 40 = 240	01 × 40 = 40
Maintain- ability	10 × 30 = 300	30 × 30 = 900	15 × 30 = 450	20 × 30 = 600
Acceler- ation	14 × 15 = 210	21 × 15 = 315	07 × 15 = 105	29 × 15 = 435
Depreci- ation	40 × 10 = 400	37 × 10 = 370	43 × 10 = 430	47 × 10 = 470
Comfort	90 × 5 = 450	60 × 5 = 300	75 × 5 = 375	80 × 5 = 400
	Total 1960	2365	1600	1945

It would therefore appear that the best or optimal truck to buy is the Maximin, even though it is not the least expensive buy. In accordance with the implications of the concept of *rationality* as defined by Kepner and Tregoe and others, the best decision to make is the one which the information clearly indicates that the value or utility is maximized, according to the attributes selected.[2]

SUMMARY

Decision theory has general applications in the selection of a course of action among competing alternatives. Basically, it deals with, among other things, an analytical framework for deciding how decision makers can make their decision more rational in the context of the relevant information and

[2] Charles H. Kepner and Benjamin B. Tregoe, *op. cit.*

criteria available. Many decision makers maintain that they make their choices on the basis of intuition. Decision theory, as used here, utilizes the objective data and intuition in the model to aggregate both into an overall preference measure that is meaningful to the decision maker and others involved in the decision. Thus decisions become an integration of the logic and intuition.

There are several advantages of using such a framework for decisions. Some of these are listed here.

1. It forces the decision maker (or subordinates) to come to grips with the important issues of the decision as embodied in the criteria.

2. It allows the combined intuition and experience of the decision maker to be brought to bear selectively on different parts of a decision problem, separately.

3. It provides a springboard for argumentation of hard data with intuitive feelings concerning the attributes and their relative importance.

4. It forces the decision maker to analytically break the decision problem into smaller components.

5. It provides a lineal rationale for the decision in question, as well as a basis for communicating the results to others. If the president of your corporation were to ask why the Maximin truck was purchased, the response could be a summary of the attributes, weights, measures, and the final sums. The ability to supply such a definitive answer will aid the communications between both superiors and subordinates.

6. It provides a formula that allows the separate judgments about attributes and alternatives to be aggregated into an overall preference score for each prospective alternative under consideration.

SKILL DEVELOPERS

1. You are confronted with a decision as to what restaurant you will dine at this evening. Your alternatives are:
   a. Steak House.
   b. Seafood Restaurant.
   c. Chinese Restaurant.
   The average price of a steak dinner at the Steak House is $8.50 per person. The average price of a Seafood dinner is $6.50, while the average price of an equivalent Chinese dinner is $5.00, including egg roll. Your budget for the meal for two is $25.00. Rate the entertainment value of the three restaurants on a five-point scale. (See the reference under "comfort" in car example of the text.) Rate "satisfaction" and "distance" in the same way. The distance to the Chinese Restaurant is 50 miles. It is 30 miles to the Seafood Restaurant which is at the beach, and 25 miles to the Steak House. Devise your own scale for "satisfaction."
   Use the rational decision model in the text to determine the proper choice for you, the decision maker.
2. List, rank, and weight five attributes you feel are most important in the following three decision situations:
   a. The promotion of a sales representative to sales manager.
   b. Whether to buy or lease a business car.
   c. What career paths are most appropriate for you.
3. You are faced with a decision to hire a subcontractor for a large contract. Three subcontracting firms have submitted proposals that meet the general specifications of the proposed project. The constraints on the decision problem are:
   a. The contract is budgeted not to exceed $150,000.
   b. No subcontractor can be awarded the project unless

his ratio of current assets to current liabilities exceeds
1.5.

c. A premium will be placed on the assignment of key
personnel who are experienced in the type of project
at issue. Construct an analytical decision model for
subcontractors A, B, and C. Use the above listed constraints. Also develop your own attribute scales for the
remaining criteria.

d. The subcontractor's reputation.

e. Your ability to communicate with him on important
issues, and reach mutually satisfactory agreements.
The following data may be relevant to the decision:

Company	Bid Price	Criteria Current Ratio	Average Experience
Company A	$ 98,000	1.6	8 years
Company B	$110,000	2.3	12 years
Company C	$112,000	3.1	15 years

Justify to your management why you selected the company you did.

PANEL DISCUSSION

Ed: How would this panel suggest that management should go about teaching other managers a process for making more effective decisions? How would you go about it, panel? Would you teach it as an analytical process or as an intuitive process, or both?

Annette: I think there is merit in teaching a step-by-step analytic process for decision making in some types of situations I face in business. For example, I have found systematic decision processes very useful in finding the cause of malfunction of hardware being tested for use in satellite systems, and then deciding what to do about it.

I feel that there are many quantifiable factors that can, and should, be evaluated, weighed and compared in arriving at a final decision, either rework, redesign, replace, etc. This is the type of situation we referred to earlier as an objective decision-making environment. I think that in a situation like this you should decide as linearly as possible, using every bit of data and history that you can muster. I think the situation is particularly factual and should be dealt with on a non-intuitive basis.

Ed: Annette, a decision that can be anticipated like the one to which you have alluded is also referred to as a programmed decision, as well as being objective.

Rich: But one person must say yes, or no, to that, Annette. And if the decision was totally linear, you could simply feed it all into a preprogrammed computer to make the decision, and absolutely no one would have to be accountable. Right?

Annette: No! One person must sign his name to the bottom line of a letter making a final recommendation. That person must make his decision from the position of maximum information after sifting through and evaluating an extremely technical data base. I think, therefore, he can profitably use a sequential process of evaluating the performance of a piece of hardware against appropriately weighted requirements or criteria in a proposed space flight. This system of evaluation might be based upon the results of prior testing of the hardware in simulated environments. The reason why a sequential process is so applicable in this case is that the important factors can be laid out and evaluated one by one very easily. How well each alternative piece of hardware scores against those requirements can be judged from other data at hand. Some kind of total score or performance for each piece of hardware can then be totaled and compared with a similar total scores or pay-offs on other pieces of hardware. Although intuition is still involved, its role is reduced to a minimum in this type of environment.

However, in other situations like the case of deciding whether or not I should transfer to Washington, D.C. from Los Angeles, the nature of the decision is entirely different. It involves such an immense set of complex and intangible factors that I think it is impossible to try to evaluate it analytically. Not only are there an infinite number of factors, but many of them are unconscious.

Ed: However, please keep in mind the fact that just because a decision process is systematic does not imply the absence of intuition. Intuition and analysis are not antithetical. It is probably a matter of degree. Of course there may be a point at which a difference in degree becomes a difference in kind.

Rich: If all decisions could be reduced to a very linear process, I feel that there would be absolutely no need for me in my organization.

Harvey: Annette, is the distinction you're drawing between the hardware example and the example of moving to Washington, D.C. based on a difference between a risk situation where you have some knowledge of the probabilities involved and an uncertainty situation where you have hopelessly inadequate data about relevant outcomes?

Annette: Exactly. Where you have some idea of the historical probabilities, a step-by-step evaluation procedure can be useful. In the total uncertainty situation, something happens in my brain that I can't even define. Somehow, intuitively, I make what I feel is the right choice.

Ed: Annette. I hear you acknowledging that it really seems like an unconscious process.

Annette: Yes. It somehow happens unconsciously, or at least subconsciously.

Hal: I see another significant difference between those two situations arising out of the level of emotional involvement you have in each situation. Annette, it seems like you're saying that when you're involved emotionally in the decision, you rely more on your intuition. It seems to me like you're saying that you won't quantify it, not that you can't evaluate its goodness or badness.

Harvey: Good or bad are subjective words used to describe an outcome. If I could get you to operationally define those terms relative to your own set of attributes, I could get you to tell me whether the outcome of your decision was either one way or the other. But I would assume every decision has an outcome, and that outcome somehow relates to certain criteria the decision maker feels are important. And therefore the outcome is either good or bad. And that, furthermore, the confidence, and perhaps even the skill, with which the decision maker makes decisions is somehow built up in accordance with that experience with making good or bad decisions.

Ken: I've got a feeling that I would like to get out on the table that's related to how, and what, to teach decision makers. I disagree with the position taken by some members at this table. I agree with Len and have come to the conclusion that all the knowing processes that are involved in good decision making are analytical.

Len: Yes, but Len didn't say that. I believe that there is a way of obtaining knowledge that is nonanalytical and that's what we call intuition.

Rich: A systematic approach to problem solving and decision making is useful but I think there is also merit in a hunch approach.

Ed: Ken is suggesting the hypothesis that all decision making, or at least all good decision making, is basically analytical and therefore, the way to teach decision making is to increase the decision maker's analytical skill. Do you agree?

Rich: I can answer by offering an alternative hypothesis of my own. It's a little abstract but try this on for size: all decisions are made intuitively and are subsequently understood or communicated analytically.

Ken: Everyone is confronted with decision making but business presumably pays more to people who rise to the challenge of making decisions than to other people who avoid making them. What is it about those people, those top executives, or the process they use?

Ed: Ken, I think we're confusing the issue. There are two distinct issues involved. One issue is how do top executives make decisions. The other is how do you and the members of this panel make their decisions. As a panel we can only speculate about the former issue. But we can introduce our own experience as evidence to reach tentative conclusions about the latter issue.

Incidentally, there is an excellent article in *Fortune Magazine* entitled, "How Businessmen Make Decisions"[3] which provides some evidence to the fact that top executives really don't know how they make decisions. Our task then, Ken, is to try to distill our experiences into some meaningful guidelines that might offer insight into improving decision processes.

Our discussion has focused on the distinction between intuitive and systematic decision making. Is decision making a fairly stable sequential process that can be neatly divided into a progression of say 10 steps which, if adhered to in some less-than-totally-rigid fashion, will produce more effective decisions? If this is the case, and decision making can be reduced to a series of steps, I may be able to teach those steps to someone with the confidence that if they follow them they may make better decisions in the future. But, if it is not, if it is essentially intuitive, then I have an entirely different teaching paradigm. This is where the split in opinion usually occurs in the literature on the subject. One group maintains that decision making is mostly intuitive and cannot be taught, the other group maintains that it is analytical and can only be fostered through analytical approaches.

Hal: It seems you can also postulate the existence of a third group: the group who says there's no one process that should be used in all situations. It's better to have two resources to draw upon rather than just one.

Ed: Ken, could you share with us where you're coming from in regard to your decision-making process? What, in your opinion, is involved in good decision making.

Ken: I think one of the characteristics of a good decision maker is a person who has the ability to analytically separate out what is really important for the problem at issue. Therefore, a poor decision maker would be one who gets too many

[3] John McDonald, *loc. cit.*, pp. 84-87, and 131-133.

things involved in the analysis and confuses the decision. I don't know, maybe it's some ability to clean up or sort the data into relevant information.

Ed: Is this basically an analytical skill?

Ken: Yes. I approach it as a systematic process. A step-by-step procedure like that proposed in Chapter Four of this text for isolating the important criteria, ranking the relative importance of each criterion, and then assessing how well each alternative satisfies each of the important criteria. The best decision is then the one which accumulates the highest total score.

Annette: Yes. That's a truly linear approach all the way.

Bob: I would like to take the liberty of setting up a little step-by-step procedure that I would follow if I were approaching a decision analytically. First, I would define the problem the best I could, given the available time and money. Second, I would gather all the data I could, again within my time and cost constraints. Third, I would clean up the data and evaluate it to determine which solution was best. There's probably a fair amount of analytic skill involved in this last step.

Ken: I think that basically you've just outlined the same process that I have just described.

Rich: But that's an analytical approach. We're not having any problems with teaching an analytical approach. We're having a problem with teaching an intuitive approach.

Ken: But how can we teach intuition? I think we need to linealize, that is, define a clear-cut, step-by-step process to go through in order to effectively lay out a decision process so that it can be taught.

Rich: And, if I were to describe a lineal approach regarding the teaching of intuitive decision making the first step would be to teach the trainee to be aware of his intuition, that is, that it does *exist*. The second step would be to encourage him to *believe* that his situation will produce an answer. The third step would be to facilitate and amplify his ability to *yield* to his intuition. A fourth step would be to provide a comparative riskless environment which will *encourage* its use on certain managerial problems.

Ed: I would like to offer an alternative approach similar to the one suggested by Hal that I think avoids the rigid dichotomy inherent in Ken's versus Rich's respective styles. Let me offer a couple of tentative hypotheses that may somewhat synthesize these two positions. I don't think we have to dichotomize quite so sharply.

First of all, some people will always tend to lean more heavily towards an analytical decision-making style while others will favor a more intuitive approach. This will probably be true as long as the problem is not either extremely subjective or objective. Let us tentatively postulate that this will be a matter of the decision maker's personal style. Furthermore, most organizations need both styles in different circumstances. Let me also delineate a second synthesizing hypothesis that we consider those analytic steps just outlined by Bob and Ken as a framework for integrating the amount of intuition that fits the dictates of the individual decision maker's personal style.

Bob: Which is what happens when you're gathering the data and you have a hunch or feeling that might be relevant. You'll throw it into the pot and consider its impact on the decision.

Ed: Yes. Intuition might become operant sporadically within different steps in the series just outlined. The systematic framework could even focus the use of intuition on specific components of the problem. I would like to contrast this quasi-intuitive, quasi-lineal process with what we can, for want of better terminology, call a totally intuitive approach.

The latter approach is holistic in nature and the decision maker is not aware of any steps. He simply knows or feels what is the right thing to do, and opts to do it. Again it is not a question of which is better. It is more difficult to justify a totally intuitive decision.

Len: I see the quasi-intuitive, quasi-sequential process you've outlined as working a little differently. I do see it as a process you go through step-by-step. I gather some facts to define the problem, and then I may gather some more facts to shed further light on the problem, but sometimes I get blocked at that point because I can't find an acceptable solution. At that point the analytical process stops. That's where intuition becomes active.

Ed: Then, what I hear you saying is that when you get blocked or reach an impasse at some point in the lineal process, intuition gets you through the eye of the needle, the "stick point."

Len: Yes.

Annette: Yes. In other words, intuition is useful when a neat step-by-step process is confounded or overwhelmed by the especially complicated nature of the situation.

Len: Yes! The process just comes to a halt!

Ed: I hear Len and Annette saying when the lineal processes bogs down, they revert to intuition. Now this question is addressed to Ken, who by this time, I suspect, favors an analytic approach. Ken, what would you do if the lineal process bogged down?

Ken: I would look for something else that would perpetuate the analytic process. If I'm trying to make a recommendation as to where to locate a plant and the results of an extensive analytical decision process came out to a halt, I'm going to look for more other data that will give me some new direction.

Ed: Ken, what I hear you doing is manifesting your strong style preference for an analytic approach. What you have, in fact, done is to experientially define what is called your personal decision-making style in terms of the process you use.[4]

[4] William T. Morris, "Matching Decision Aids with Intuitive Styles," *Decision Making: Creativity, Judgment, and Systems*, Henry S. Brinkers, ed., (Columbus, Ohio: Ohio State University Press, 1972), pp. 190-204.

five

Who Will Riddle Me a Riddle of the How and the Why of Hunches

Out of the dreaming past,
with its legends of steaming seas and gleaming glaciers,
mountains that moved and suns that glared,
emerges this creature, man—the latest phase in a continuing
process that stretches back to the beginning of life.
His is the heritage of all that has lived;
he still carries the vestiges of snout and fangs and claws
of species long since vanished;
he is the ancestor of all that is yet to come.

Don't regard him lightly—he is you.

Anonymous
Foreseeing the Unforeseeable

LEARNING OBJECTIVES

When you have completed this chapter you should begin to understand the following:

1. Intuition can be understood as a cognitive faculty of the mind that has access to the inner, unconscious world within us.
2. That intuition tends to function suddenly and holistically, grasping the whole of a situation at once.
3. How intuition can be implemented in a systematic decision model.
4. That in order to develop intuitive skills, a decision maker must learn to:
   a. *Listen for* intuition.
   b. *Rely on* intuition.
   c. *Accept* intuition as a valuable clue.
   d. *Yield to* or flow with intuition.
   e. *Be sensitive* to whatever fears or anxieties he might experience when exploring the peaks and valleys associated with intuitive flashes.

GLOSSARY

Freudian Associated with or developed by the famous Austrian psychiatrist Sigmund Freud.

Jungian Associated with or developed by the famous Swiss psychiatrist Carl Gustav Jung.

ESP Estrasensory perception. Sometimes it is called PSI.

Multidimensional Attribute Evaluation Considering attributes of facets simultaneously. The decision model in Chapter Four is a multidimensional attribute evaluation model.

Principle of the Division of Labor   The economic principle that specialization in one function or task increases efficiency.

Introvert   Someone who is inward going and introspective in contrast with an extrovert, someone who is outward going from the self.

In earlier chapters of the text and in the dialogue, we have repeatedly alluded to the fact that management decision making often involves substantial use of intuition. Let us see if we can offer some documentation for this position among top executives and extrepreneurs.

It is no secret among many executives and entrepreneurs that much of the elegant, new analytic paraphernalia that can be used to augment a systematic approach to decision making is often as helpful to the decision as a pencil sharpener. Management expert C. I. Shartle remarks that "most decisions are made on the basis of incomplete evidence. Facts may not be available; or, there may not be sufficient time or staff assistance, to uncover or assemble them. Thus, a good executive must be a good guesser. Some executives have a reputation for being uncanny in making the 'right' decision without apparent evidence."[1] Business executive Chester Barnard calls hunch decision making "non-logical" decision making.[2]

Charles Kemmons Wilson, founder and Chairman of the Board of Holiday Inn Inc., who frequently selected sites for new locations, says, "looking for land is like going on an Easter egg hunt, and sometimes you find the golden egg."[3] He confesses that he sometimes rejects a prospective site after weeks of analytic study simply because "he doesn't

---

[1] C. I. Shartle, *Executive Performance and Leadership*, (Englewood Cliffs, N.J.: Prentice-Hall, 1956).

[2] Chester I. Barnard, *The Function of the Executive*, (Cambridge: Harvard University Press, 1956).

[3] "The Rapid Rise of the Host with the Most," *Time*, June 12, 1972.

" I CAN'T TELL WHETHER IT'S INTUITION OR JUST
PLAIN INDIGESTION!"

like the smell of it."[4] Says Fletcher Byrom, president of
Kopper Company, "If you have well-developed intuition,
don't be afraid to use it. I have found that some of the
most horrible mistakes we made came after I ignored my
intuition under the pressure of what looked, at the time,

4 Ibid.

like unshakeable evidence."[5] Since intuitive hunches seem
to comprise such a vital part of the decision-making process
of top management, let us proceed to examine their nature
more carefully.

WHAT IS "RIGHT" MAY BE LEFT!

What is a hunch? It is a strong, intuitive impression about
something, or about something that will happen. A hunch is
a signal or flash from the unconscious and the very basis of
intuitive decision making. In an interview, Buckminster Fuller once commented that, "everybody has intuition very,
very powerfully. But most of us today are so quickly frus-
trated about things, that we learn not to listen to our intuition."[6] During the same interview, Fuller also remarked
that until the 1950s "intuition was literally a dirty word in
the sciences."

At first, many so-called management scientists fantasized
that their primary professional goal was to eliminate the use
of intuition in decision making. Many executives will even
try to hide the intuitive basis of their decisions by concocting elaborate rationale to bolster the credibility of their
decisions in the eyes of peers.

The Dark Side of Knowing

However, there is something about intuition and how it
seems to work that is always slightly beyond our best analytical grasp. There is something in it that always seems to
remain hidden and mysterious. It is like trying to capture a

[5] F. L. Byrom, "A Top Executive's Advice: Hang Loose," *Dun's
Review*, September, 1969.

[6] Beverly Russel, "An Interview with R. Buckminister Fuller,"
House and Garden, May 1972.

mirage in the desert: no matter how swiftly we approach it, it always manages to elude us at the last moment!

Let us try to reach an understanding of the subject of intuition slowly from the more solid analytical ground of definition. Webster defines intuition as "the art or process of coming into direct knowledge, or certainty, without reasoning or inference; immediate conviction, or cognizance without rational thought; revelation by insight, or innate knowledge."[7] The root of the word derives from the Latin word *intueri*, which means *to look inward*. In other words, it denotes a form of inward perception. Our physical senses of sight, hearing, and so forth, provide faculties for perceiving the *outside* world. Intuition is a faculty for perceiving what happens in our *inside* world, presumably in the *unconscious*. Robert Ornstein's conception of how the brain operates was discussed in Chapter Two. Ornstein suggests that the brain is divided into two loosely connected parts. One half of the brain, usually the left half in right-handed people, tends to operate in what may be called a *real time* mode. Real time is what we usually experience as normal conscious time, chronological, or clock time. This left brain tends to specialize in rational or logical thought processes— so-called lineal processes. The other half of the brain appears to be reserved for the less conscious, more diffuse, perhaps unconscious thinking normally associated with speculation and imagination. There seems to be less direct contact and voluntary control over the use of the data and functioning of this portion of the brain.

BUT WHERE DOES IT COME FROM?

If knowledge can be thought of as data, or information in the brain, the question naturally arises, what is the *source*

[7] *Webster's New International Dictionary of the English Language,*

of the so-called intuitive knowledge that manifests itself in hunches?

The Freudian Dust Bin

There are at least three hypothetical explanations of the source of this knowledge. The first one is what we call the Freudian "dust bin"[8] theory. This theory proceeds from the assumption that the humans have the capacity to collect more data from an experience than they usually want or need. The fractional amount of data that gets into consciousness is both quantitatively and qualitatively the bare minimum that is needed for survival. The rest, which does not get through the sieve separating the conscious and unconscious world, is dumped in a kind of "dust bin" of accumulated experience for possible later retrieval. The brain probably performs a kind of selective filtering function, sorting out the data of present experience which is needed for survival. Our conscious perception, the mental stuff of which we are aware, defines *how* we perceive, or see, the decision-making situation. But what happens to all that leftover stuff that does not get through into consciousness? Where is it stored? We could assume that much of this information is probably dumped into dusty storage bins in the recesses of the right brain. It may be instructive to note also that since it was not catalogued, organized, or otherwise collated that the retrieval of this information is probably not a straightforward process. We cannot expect our brains to provide us with a neatly indexed data dump of information on

Second Ed., Unabridged, W. A. Neilson, ed. (Springfield, Mass.: G. & C. Merriam Co., Publishers, 1953) p. 1304.

[8] "Movies, The Story of C. G. Jung," "Face to Face," and "Discussions with Dr. C. G. Jung." Carl G. Jung, "Approaching the Unconscious," *Man and His Symbols,* (Garden City, N.Y.: Doubleday & Co., Inc., 1964) pp. 18-103.

command. What this assumption means is that stored somewhere in the caverns of our brain, probably the right brain,
is a vast amount of data that might become available if we
could arrange to coax it out and get access to it. A related
speculative tangent involves the concept of shifts in consciousness or awareness. If we could learn to facilitate a
process whereby our ordinary rational mode of consciousness was deflected, altered, or expanded, then perhaps this
information could be made available for decision making.
We will return to this later in the chapter.

Larger Than Life

The second explanation for the origin of intuitive insight
is an extension of what we have just described as the Freudian "dust bin" theory. We can call this second explanation
the Jungian "larger-than-life" theory.[9] This theory is based
on C. G. Jung's concept of a collective unconscious that all
human beings share. According to this hypothesis, Freud's
concept of a personal dust bin of unconscious experience
represents only the tip of the proverbial iceberg. Jung and
his disciples maintain that there is evidence in man of a vast
psychic residue of collective human experience reflecting the
evolutionary struggle of our species for survival. New thoughts
that have never been conscious before arise from the dark
depths of this unconscious past and occasionally become
visible like new species of fish from the bosom of the ocean.

ESP

A third possible explanation for hunches originates from
parapsychology rather than psychiatry. This may be loosely

[9] Ibid.

called the "ESP theory of intuition." According to this school of thought, intuition arises as a by-product of so-called extra-sensory experience.[9a]

Regardless of the particular hypothesis or explanation we prefer to choose (and they are certainly not mutually exclusive), the essential point is that unconscious data, from one source or another, can be tapped and combined in some novel fashion with the data of immediate experience to produce what we call a hunch.

The simplest way to look at intuition is as a cognitive or knowing faculty of the mind whereby we understand things suddenly and holistically rather than in a piecemeal manner, as in analytical or intellectual understanding.

ZAP! A SUDDEN FLASH OF INTUITION!

Intuition tends to work *suddenly* and *holistically*.[10] It seems to instantaneously furnish the problem solver with a sometimes total shift in consciousness—an entirely fresh perspective. This experience is well documented and is referred to as the "A-ha Phenomenon."[10a] In order to attempt to illustrate by analogy how this aspect of intuition works, consider the cube in Figure 5-1. You may perceive the cube as a transparent cube with the corners marked A and B in the lower front, and the corners marked C and D in the lower rear. From this perspective you will view the cube from the front, slightly above. You may also see the cube with the corners marked A and B in the lower back of the cube, and the

[9a] Douglas Dean, John Mihalasky, Sheila Ostrander, and Lynn Shroeder, *Executive ESP*, (Englewood Cliffs, N.J.: Prentice-Hall, 1974), pp. 36–44.

[10] Robert E. Ornstein, *op. cit.*, pp. 144–178.

[10a] Hudson Hoagland, *loc. cit.*, p. 1.

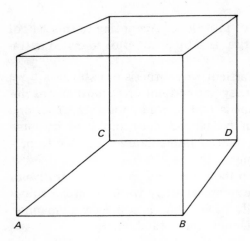

Figure 5-1. A multiperspective cube.

corners marked *C* and *D* in the lower front. From this perspective you will view the cube from the front, slightly
below. If you already know the cube, as a cube with the
corners marked *A* and *B* in the front, you may experience a
difficulty in altering your awareness. May we suggest that
you invert Figure 5-1, turning it upside down. Stare at it for
some minutes. Suddenly you may see it another way; that is,
as a cube with the corners labeled *A* and *B* appearing in the
lower rear, and the corners, *C* and *D* in the lower front.
Only now, because it is inverted, you will visualize it upside down. Your visual perception might even shift a third
way. You could perceive it as the aerial view of a cube with
C and *D* at the top front, and *A* and *B* at the bottom front.
These sudden shifts in awareness are meant to simulate the
changes in consciousness that often accompany intuitive
flashes of insight. They may alter a decision maker's entire
perspective on a problem. Please also make mental note of
the fact that these various ways of knowing or seeing the
cube are in conflict with each other. You cannot see them

both at the same time. Frequently you will hear people arguing about the way they see the problem. If such dramatic shifts in consciousness should occur in a decision problem as the result of an intuitive flash, then this may help explain why a decision maker might suddenly shift perspective on a problem and take an entirely new tack that seems to be in conflict with the apparent implications of the data that has been accumulated.

Since the data source that provides the basis for intuition may be stored in a chaotic or disorganized way, the conscious rational mind would have to provide the function for translating or converting intuition into statements that could be communicated or verbalized to others. In this sense, reason is the companion of intuition. The logical part of the brain can verify the credibility of an intuitive hunch before the hunch becomes incorporated into our acceptable knowledge about a particular decision-making situation. Intuition can therefore play a very important role in searching for solutions whose relevance may not be readily apparent from the data of immediate experience.

BUT HOW DOES IT FEEL?

What is frequently referred to as the *gambler's hunch, feminine intuition*, the *manager's gut feel* are all pragmatic terms describing similar intuitive processes. The inspiration of the artist, the breakthrough of the inventor, and the sudden visionary flash of the mathematician are all examples of the influence of intuition in problem solving. The experiences of generating hunches from the unconscious is well documented. Friedrich Wilhelm Nietzche in *Ecce Home* gives a dramatic description of how he experiences intui-

A BROKERAGE HOUSE RECEIVES AN ORDER FROM
CONRAD HILTON TO BUY WALDORF-ASTORIA BONDS

tion: "The notion of revelation describes the conditions
quite simply; by which I mean that something profoundly
convulsive and disturbing suddenly becomes visible and
audible . . . one hears—one does not seek; one takes—one
does not ask who gives: a thought flashes out like light-

ening."[11]   Alfred Binet, in describing how he facilitates intuition, reports, "I find that images appear only if we give our ideas uncontrolled freedom—when we are dreaming while awake. As soon as full consciousness, voluntary consciousness returns, images weaken, darken; they seem to withdraw to some unknown region."[12] Francis Galton, in his book *Inquiries Into Human Faculty*, bears witness to the relationship between the unconscious source of intuition and its experience in consciousness. He says, "there seems to be a presence-chamber in my mind where full consciousness holds court, and where two or three ideas are at the same time given an audience, and an antichamber full of more or less allied ideas, which is situated just beyond the full ken of consciousness. Out of this antichamber, the ideas most nearly allied to those in the presence-chamber appear to be summoned in a mechanically logical way, and to have their turn in audience."[13] The poet A. E. Hausman in *The Name and Nature of Poetry* describes how intuition will intrude on one's serenity with sometimes sudden and unexpected force: "As I went along, thinking nothing in particular, only looking at things around me, and following the progress of the seasons, there would flow into my mind, with sudden and unaccountable emotion, sometimes a line or two of verse, sometimes a whole stanza at once."[14] Amy Lowell seems to corroborate this experience. Commenting on the serendipity of a hunch she once said, "the idea dropped into the subconscious, like a letter into a mailbox."[15] The author, Thomas Wolfe, in his "The Story of a Novel," paints a dramatic picture of how the idea of a

[11] Don Faubin, ed., "You and Creativity," Vol. 25, No. 3, *Kaiser Aluminum News*, (Oakland, California: Kaiser Aluminum & Chemical Corporation, 1968), p. 9.
[12] Don Faubin, *op. cit.*, p. 10.
[13] Ibid.
[14] Don Faubin, op. cit., p. 125.
[15] Ibid.

story emerges from his intuition: "It seemed that I had inside me, swelling and gathering all the time, a huge black cloud, and that this cloud was loaded with electricity, pregnant, crested with a kind of hurricane violence that could not be held in check much longer; that the moment was approaching fast when it must break. Well, all I can say is that the storm did break. It came in a torrent and it is not over yet."[16] Henry Eyring in "Scientific Creativity" reports on the ability of intuition to organize ideas out of the chaos of the unconscious: "the living system here is exercising its ability to integrate and organize a pattern out of formlessness, an achievement which rational thought, being somewhat removed from its primitive living source and bound with habit and convention, may be incapable of doing."[17] In remarking on unconsciousness as the source of intuition, George J. Seidel in "The Crisis of Creativity" says, "The disorganized chaos contained within the unconscious is something like the carbon molecule. This is the molecule from which scientists generally feel that life derived and evolved. In the carbon molecule there is a loose association between electrons, one which permits a wide variety of synthesis. The unconscious represents the same sort of chaos; it represents a loose association of experiences, images, psychic events, which can be linked together unconsciously in a wide variety of ways."[18]

The Business World and Intuition

Business executives are usually more blunt and less grandiose in talking about their encounters with intuition. In the first place, they usually call intuition a hunch, probably be-

[16] Ibid.
[17] Don Faubin, *op. cit.*, p. 14.
[18] Ibid.

cause of the frequent association of the term intuition with the concept of feminine intuition. For example, there is a well-known story concerning the hotel magnate, Conrad Hilton.

During World War II, Hilton got a hunch that he should snap up Waldorf-Astoria bonds at $4\frac{1}{2}$ cents on the dollar. Most other hotel executives in the East thought the bonds worthless. Duncan Harris, who was the president of a large real estate firm located in the East, permitted Hilton to eavesdrop on a telephone call that he placed with his broker concerning the profitability of the Waldorf bonds as a possible investment. The unnamed broker was quoted by Hilton as remarking that "some wild man from the West has forced them up to 8 cents. We're unloading them by the bushel. This is the first time in years anyone in the hotel business has believed in Santa Claus." Nevertheless, Hilton and a small group of skeptical investors reluctantly backed "Connie's hunch." A short time later, hotel securities boomed and the "wild man from the West" liquidated the securities he had purchased for $4\frac{1}{2}$ cents at 85 cents. This wild man's hunch had reaped almost half a million dollars on the basis of $22,000 in front-end money. Hilton himself confesses that he has been accused more than once of playing his hunches, and he also remarked that he "further believes that most people have them whether they follow them or not." He also makes the interesting point that the key to developing your intuition is *listening for it.*[19]

Then, there is a well-known Alaska "North Slope"[20] incident. In the spring of 1969, the so-called "North Slope" oil lands in Alaska went up for bid. The Wall Street Journal

[19] Conrad Hilton, *Be My Guest*, (Englewood Cliffs, N.J.: Prentice-Hall, 1957).

[20] Roger Benedict, "North Slope Gamble Oil Land Bin in Alaska Took Study, Guesswork, and a Hunch." *Wall Street Journal*, Nov. 17, 1969.

wryly referred to the bidding as "the North Slope Gamble."
After the bidding was over, Amarada-Hess-Getty Oil Combine landed the best piece of oil land: 6 square miles of
perspective drill sights for about 73 million dollars. It was
revealed later that Amarada-Hess-Getty nearly dropped the
ball. At the eleventh hour, the weekend just prior to when
the contracts were awarded, they suddenly upped their bid.
They won the bid by what was considered a fractional mar-
gin above their nearest rival. Leon Hess, in offering an explanation as to why he had upped his bid at the last minute,
said, "I suddenly had a hunch."

Alfred P. Sloan, a former president of General Motors,
characterizes William C. Durrant, the founder of General
Motors, as a man who "would proceed on a course of action guided solely, as far as I could tell, by some intuitive
flash of brilliance. He never felt obliged to make an engineering search for the facts." Sloan, who himself has been referred to as one of the greatest organizing geniuses of American
business, has remarked "the final act of business judgment
is intuitive."[21]

BUT WHAT GOOD IS IT?

If intuition and hunches play such a key role in management
decision making, why then does the literature on decision making deal with them so superficially? Why have management
analysts and writers on decision making refused to take a
good hard look at these phenomena? Can intuitive decision
making be facilitated or developed the way that weight
lifting develops a muscle? Can managers really be trained to
make better hunch decisions? One thing strikes us as singu-

[21] Douglas Dean, John Michalasky, *op. cit.*, pp. 4-5.

larly important. Many of the highly structured, or systematic, approaches to decision making have a very pious ring to them. They seem to imply that all intuition is bad or unsophisticated, or both, and should be discarded by the decision maker. As a matter of fact, young management scientists and operations researchers not too infrequently pursue with Messianic fervor a mission to free business from the yoke of intuition and other forms of unscientific leftovers from our Neanderthal roots. We feel that such a pseudo-analytical conversion is impossible. Too, much of the evidence seems to indicate that, depending on the individual decision maker and the decision problem, the implementation of varying degrees of intuition may prove quite fruitful in specific situations. We view this conclusion not as novel and as yet untested specualtion, but rather as a fairly straightforward interpretation of the data. We suggest that there are some decisions that suffer from such a deficiency in hard data that, if time or cost does not permit the gathering of more data, the decision maker must of necessity rely on intuition. However, what is even more important, and much less understood, is the crucial role mentioned in Chapters Two and Four that intuition can play in perfecting a rational or systematic approach to decision making.

Complementary Roles

Perhaps one of the most knotty aspects involved in an analytical approach to any complicated business decision is the problem of choosing, bottom line, the best alternative from the several possibilities, all things considered. Each alternative must be evaluated against several conflicting decision criteria or attributes of varying importance to the decision. This is particularly true when the criteria or attributes represent sharply conflicting trade-offs; that is, the more you get of one attribute, the less you automatically get of another. For example, taking the example of Chapter Four, suppose that we face a trade-off between initial cost and comfort. Each of these attributes or decision criteria represents a one-dimensional scale on which intuition can focus very efficiently. The principle involved is this: *It is far simpler to compare or rank the cars intuitively one attribute at a time, and then to aggregate or combine these single intuitive evaluations into an overall preference score using an analytical approach.* If we attempt to simultaneously perform an intuitive evaluation of the autos with regard to all attributes, the factors involved in the combined evaluation multiply exponentially with the number of attributes. This evaluation may be difficult to perform or communicate.

In other words, a good analytical process can facilitate intuition in two ways. First of all, it permits intuition to focus on the evaluation of one-dimensional attributes. It also permits intuition to evaluate each alternative against each attribute one at a time. It is then rather easy to explain to someone else why we decided the way we did. Secondly, a good analytical process permits the decision maker to see how the quasi-intuitively assigned values and weights in a linear decision process are aggregated into an overall preference or utility score on which to base the decision. Similar problems also arise for the manager deciding where to locate a new plant, how to change methods of depreciation, and in fact, in making nearly all important decisions. It is important to emphasize how intuition can in this way play a vitalizing role in rational decision making. By the same token, the logic involved in the systematic approach can provide the valuable service of validating intuition.

To repeat the crucial principle, using unaided intuition on single attributes and alternatives in a multidimensional attribute evaluation model is probably more effective. In a sense, what we are doing is linealizing the implementation of intuition with supporting data that will also assist in communicating it. The process of focusing intuition along one-dimensional attribute scales is what R. T. Eckenrode calls "the principle of the division of labor."[22]

Logic works analytically, piecing together the elements of the large decision puzzle. If the complementary mode of consciousness, intuition, is developed, knowledge of the decision problem becomes more complete. This is the thrust to the story of the blind men and the elephant mentioned in Chapter Two.

BUT WHAT CAN I DO ABOUT IT?

If indeed, as we have suggested, intuition is useful in decision making, the first question that naturally arises is: How can it be developed? The first step to accomplish this, must be taken by the individual decision maker. It is what Conrad Hilton alluded to. The decision maker must learn to *listen* for intuition. If the person does not listen for intuition and hunches, he or she cannot expect to experience them. This is admittedly an absurdly simple but amazingly potent suggestion. It is a subtle but very important inward turning, or introspective process. It amounts to the task of becoming a part-time *introvert*, listening for intuitive signals. The art of learning to listen for intuition is as difficult to develop as the art of learning to listen, really listen, to what others are saying. The process is also heavily laden with symbolic significance because it is an implicit *act of faith* in the existence of intuition and hunches. Why would you, so to speak, listen, if there was nothing there to listen for?

[22] R. T. Eckenrode, "Weighting Multiple Criteria," *Management Science*, 12:3 (1965), pp. 180–192.

The second thing a decision maker must do in order to use intuition effectively is to sincerely believe that unconscious thinking will deliver meaningful answers to problems through intuition. This commitment to intuition is also loaded with symbolic importance. It amounts to an explicit *act of hope*, or optimism, in the power of intuition. It is the belief that you will eventually get an answer if you sincerely believe one will be forthcoming.

A third thing a decision maker must do is to be prepared to *accept* whatever solution intuition should provide in solving a problem. This sense of acceptance of "whatever will be, will be," is based on a sense of equanimity and objectivity. It is a willingness to entertain any solution. It runs counter to bigotry, bias, or rigidity in the decison maker. This openness to intuition is also far more significant symbolically than it might seem on the surface. It is like an implicit *act of charity* to the unconscious solutions that are presented by the decision maker's intuition.

As a mnemonic device, we might call these first three principles for facilitating intuition, the principles of faith, hope, and charity.

The fourth step is related to the third. It involves coming to terms with the personal fear that may be involved in letting the unconscious contents of intuition emerge into consciousness. This could be experienced as an anxiety-producing or insecure feeling for some because we are risking that unconscious fears and fantasies which we have repressed, will surface and make their presence felt. The difficulty with opening up the door to the unconscious is that we may let out more than we bargained for. Not only may we get some interesting and novel hunches, we may also encounter repressed fears, dreadful fantasies, and other goblins associated with those hunches that we have done our best to avoid. In other words, if you start listening too hard to your intuition, perhaps you may hear more than you really wanted to hear. This could be quite a fearful experience for some. If intuition is to be developed, however, this risk must be faced.

The fifth step involved in the process of facilitating intuition is the act of *yielding to,* or *going with* the intuition that has been heard. This process is probably one of the most difficult and subtle concepts of all to communicate verbally. We might describe it as successively *getting into* the intuition or hunch—deeper and deeper and deeper—*flowing with it,* so to speak. For example, if I have a hunch that a recent decision is incorrect and I yield to it or flow with it, then I may begin to entertain the implications of the hunch seriously, giving it more power or credence. Eventually, I may dig up further analytical support for the suspected error. What is most important is *not* to summarily reject or repress it.

The foregoing steps are merely suggestions or guidelines indicating how individual decision makers can initiate the process of education for their own intuition.

DEVELOPING INTUITION IN MANAGERS

Let us also briefly discuss how superiors might assist subordinates in management with the development of intuition in the realm of decision making. The long-run importance of this assistance can be crucial to the manager's career. As the middle manager moves slowly up the hierarchical ladder of executive leadership, the need for intuition in top-level decision making becomes more pronounced. No longer is the manager faced with the pressure to justify decisions analytically. The individual must simply respond to the overwhelming pressure to make the right decision regardless of the basis. Unless management faces the responsibility of cultivating a promising manager's intuition (which is usually called judgment), it must face the fact that the person will probably fall victim to the working of the Peter Principle: he or she will stop growing at the highest level of intuitive incompetancy.

How, therefore, can management proceed toward developing a manager's judgment in decision making? A straightforward oversimplified answer is *through feedback with low downside risk*. Let us explain. First of all, management must refrain from deriding or derrogating the use of unaided intuition in making judgments in appropriate decision-making circumstances. Its implementation can be facilitated in two ways, depending upon the nature of the situation.

One way for management to encourage the use of intuition is to give the trainee the opportunity to use personal judgment in making subjective decisions in comparatively low-risk environments. For example, when such a low-risk decision situation arises, the trainee could be encouraged to actively utilize hunches as to what is the best course of action for the company to pursue. This would assist in developing the trainee's awareness of when it is appropriate to use intuition in support of judgments and when it is not. The individual could also benefit from constructive feedback designed to enable the person to experience or grow accustomed to the effectiveness of intuition. This would have to be acted out in a decision-making environment where the downside risk of loss to the trainee is kept to a minimum. The purpose of these exercises is to initiate a feeling of confidence in the trainee concerning the value of intuition in making judgments. Once the person has made intuitive judgments, the trainee could be requested to accumulate analytical evidence in order to build further reinforcement for the credibility of intuitive inferences. Hopefully, this would have the effect of building more self-confidence in having the right hunch at the right time.

Another opportunity for management to assist the trainee in the implementation of intuition arises in decisionmaking situations that by their nature call for a systematic approach. In this situation the trainee can be encouraged to selectively use intuition in making judgments wherever it is appropriate. For example, the person can certainly use intuition in developing the weights which are a basis for the attributes in an analytical model. The trainee also has a chance to utilize intuition in concocting the values which are developed in order to compare each feasible alternative to each attribute one at a time.

In both types of situations, a partially sheltered environment is created for the decision-making trainee in which the social risk and economic loss that may result from using intuition in judgments are controlled until the trainee has cultivated his gut feeling and the requisite self-confidence. The social risk centers around an anticipated loss in self-esteem in the eyes of superiors or peers because the trainee cannot produce strong analytical support for a hunch. The economic loss is closely allied to survival threats: the fear of not being promoted, or even more drastic, the fear of being fired as a result of following intuition.

SUMMARY

Intuition is the basis of so-called hunch decision making. Although it is always slightly beyond our analytical grasp, intuition can be understood as a cognitive or knowing faculty of the mind that has access to the inner, unconscious world in each of us. It tends to function suddenly and holistically.

Intuition can be implemented effectively in the rational decision model in Chapter Four by using it, for example, in the judgments about the relative magnitude of the attribute weights. These intuitive evaluations of the weights assigned to each attribute can then be aggregated into an overall preference score for each alternative using the formula defined in the decision model. In this way, the process of intuitive evaluation is separated from the process of aggregating the evaluations.

How can the use of intuition in decision making be developed?

1. The decision maker must learn to *listen* for intuition.
2. The decision maker must learn to *depend* on intuition.
3. The decision maker must learn to *accept* hunches, whatever they are.
4. The decision maker must *come to terms* with the personal fears and anxiety that sometimes may be experienced in listening to intuition.
5. The decision maker must learn to *yield to* or *flow with* hunches.

How can managers assist trainees in the task of using intuitive judgments in decision making?

1. By creating opportunities for the exercise of intuitive judgments within a relatively low-risk environment and then giving trainees feedback on the effectiveness of their decisions.
2. By encouraging the use of intuition by trainees within an analytical framework where appropriate.

SKILL DEVELOPERS

1. What is meant by the statement that management scientists may think that their primary goal is to eliminate the use of intuition?

2. Use outside reference sources to look up the definition of Jung's "collective unconscious" and try to relate it to the discussion in the text.
3. Complete the following statements:
    a. The biggest advantage to intuitive decision making is
       _____ .
    b. The biggest advantage to systematic decision making is _____ .
    c. The biggest disadvantage to intuitive decision making is _____ .
    d. The biggest disadvantage to systematic decision making is_____ .
4. Discuss the possible relationship, if any, that might exist between hunches and extrasensory perception.
5. Imagine that a systematic decision model could be constructed for each of the following decisions:
    a. Going into a new business venture.
    b. Loaning debt money to a proprietor.
    c. Who to vote for as president of the United States.
    d. What house to buy.
    What useful part, if any, would intuition probably play in each of the above decisions? Discuss in detail.
6. Rate the Porsche 911 first, and then the Mercedes 450SL, one at a time, on a 1-10 scale, 1 being the lowest and 10 the highest. Using this attribute rating only, which would you decide to buy? What is the role of intuition in this decision?
7. What data, if any, was used in Question 6?
8. How could hard data for the decision in Assignment 6 be developed?
9. Discuss in detail the role intuition could effectively play for the car decision that was systematically approached in Chapter Four.
10. Discuss what is meant by listening to, believing in, and yielding to intuition. Discuss how could these be done.

11. What is meant by the statement, "a manager may reach the highest level of intuitive incompetency"?
12. Discuss what you personally think would be your greatest fear in using a lot of intuition in your decision-making processes.

PANEL DISCUSSION

Ed: It looks as though there are at least two types of situations, or contexts, in which decisions occur in management. One involves a substantial amount of historical or other data. Some type of sequential process is probably quite relevant in this case. The other is short of hard data, filled with ambiguity and, for this situation, the so-called crystal ball or intuitive approach appears more relevant. Now, this is fine as long as we can divide the world and its decisions into two neat stereo-typical piles: the ones with a lot of clear-cut data and the ones with ambiguous data. I'd be willing to wager that if we sat down and attempted to empirically classify decisions into these two categories we would wind up with a great big leftover pile into which most decisions fall; namely, those that have some hard data and a lot of ambiguous data. With this vast majority of typical decision problems, how would you go about facilitating a process that would enable management trainees to make better decisions?

Rich: I think a lineal or sequential process is fairly easy to teach. But, I think the use of intuition is more difficult to teach because the process seems as though it is mostly unconscious and reflexive. However, I believe that intuitive problem solving and decision making often involve what I feel are higher levels of creativity. An organization which inhibits creativity would probably also stifle the implementation of intuitive decision making. I think a truly creative organization has to allow the individual the freedom to explore his hunches and extrapolate their implications.

Ed: You mean that he has to be permitted the latitude to discover the power of his intuition?

Rich: Yes. I think that first what you have to do is to make the person conscious of his intuition. Secondly, you must give him the opportunity to experiment with that intuition.

After that, you must discuss the results of the decision-making processes he went through, and explore what could be done to improve his batting average.

Ed: Rich, have you ever experimented with some of the ideas to which you have alluded?

Rich: Yes. I have two immediate subordinates who I am trying to make more effective, intuitive decision makers. I'm actually deliberately encouraging their use of intuition. When they're finished making an intuitive judgment in a decision, I sit down with them and assist them in laying it out systematically. After I do this I ask them whether they think their decision is going to work. If they answer, yes, I'll press them to the wall and ask them how they know. They usually respond, "Well, I just know, Rich! I want you to trust me."

Ed: What I think I hear you saying, Rich, is that you subtly encourage them to yield to their intuition in a decision first. Then you gradually try to draw out the reasons why they made the decision the way they did so that they reinforce the intuition by linealizing it.

Rich: Yes, precisely.

Ed: Then, assuming they are successful, what would such a process accomplish?

Rich: Hopefully, it would begin to build their self-esteem and confidence in their intuition.

Len: Yes, and you teach them also to move freely back and forth from a more intuitive to a more analytical decision process.

Ed: You also make them conscious that their conclusion was derived intuitively. You are making a person aware of the fact that he is using his intuition.

Len: I wonder whether or not intuition is an inborn process which is uneducable? You either have it, or you don't?

Annette: I think that you can teach awareness and the utility of it. I think there are also ways of teaching a person to yield to it. I think you can even teach processes, like meditation or self-hypnosis which are oriented at amplifying the signals from it—processes that facilitate intuition.

Rich: Yes, I would agree that intuition can be facilitated, but I think that some individuals seem to be more ripe for its development.

Ed: Let me briefly refer your attention to some research that was done a few years ago at Harvard University on decision-making and problem-solving styles. The research indicated tentatively that there are two general types of managers that used distinct styles in approaching problems. These managers gave evidence of differing efficiency in the type of problems each style was more effective in solving. The recommendation from the researchers included the comment that it probably was not a good idea to try to encourage managers to switch styles. They concluded it was perhaps better to use both styles side by side in juxtaposition.

Annette: The more I reflect on our present discussion, the more I think that what intuition really is, is the ability to draw on a vast hidden data bank within the recesses of our psyche.

Ed: I'd like to suggest that there are several possible paradigms that may be relevant in discussion concerning the nature of how intuition works. One model is what I like to think of as the kind of Freudian "dust bin" model where the unconscious is thought of as a kind of old dust bin, full of unwanted data from prior experience. It is being suggested that we can retrieve information from this data bank by using intuitive processes.[23] The other model is Jungian in nature. It proceeds from the hypothesis that much of the content of the unconscious is "larger than life."[24] It assumes that the so-called collective unconscious provides an innate wellspring of buried wealth. It does not preclude the idea of the "Freudian dust bin" of experience, but it does postulate the existence of a deeper layer of broader information underneath it. Still another model proceeds from the hypothesis that some intuition derives from extra-sensory perception. But we don't have to choose one model over the other. All three of them are consistent with using intuition in decision making.

Bob: What, in your opinion, distinguishes an intuitive decision?

Rich: I think intuitive decision making is: decision making on an unconscious level, such that when it reaches the conscious level, it's unexplainable. You know, I can see where it could be dangerous, or at least risky, for a middle manager to use a lot of intuition in his decision making.

Hal: Yes, because, once again, in middle management we have to justify our decisions whether we make them intuitively or not.

Rich: I also believe you have to be in a position in the corporation with enough visibility that you can see the whole situation surrounding the decision before you can operate very effectively in an intuitive fashion.

Ed: Why do you suppose that there is evidence of so much resistance to acknowledging the use of intuition in decision making?

[23] See note 8, Chapter 5.
[24] See note 8, Chapter 5.

Rich: Perhaps it's incompatible with our values.

Ed: There's some evidence to indicate that anything that is arrived at in a rational manner, using reasonable or logical processes, is valued more highly in our culture, particularly in business.

Bill: I think it's important for managers to be aware of both approaches to making decisions. If all you have is a hammer, you will probably tend to treat everything around you like a nail because that's the only tool you have to use. If the only tool we have is reason and logic, we would tend to apply that to all decisions regardless of whether or not it may be appropriate. I suppose the relevant question is, how do you decide which tool to use in a given situation? How do you implement each tool as a process? Does it depend upon the penchant of the decision maker?

Rich: In response to all three questions, other things being equal, I favor the use of intuition and I think I can give a good example of when and how I make an intuitive decision. When I purchase a personal car, I don't go to the *Consumer Reports* so that I can compare models on the basis of criteria relating to cost or mechanical features. I see it on the street! It looks good! I know that's the car I want. It's just that simple. Now, of course, it cannot be ridiculously expensive or mechanically inferior to every other car.

Ed: I'd like to share something that relates to what we're talking about and solicit some feedback from the panel. I can indeed identify with the concept of intuitive cognition in problem solving and decision making. At times, I am conscious of the fact that I know I can rely on my unconscious to deliver the answer to various problems that I encounter in business. When I want my intuition to work for me, most of the time, sooner or later, it's there! I trust in that process enough that I will sometimes risk going ahead and make a scheduled commitment to provide answers to consulting problems even before I have as yet done much of the analytical research that will eventually support my answer. I very seldom get into a bind following this path, and if I did, I'm certain I would use a different approach.

Rich: I can identify very strongly with that process. Of course, I guess up to this time, I labeled this as the ability to think and make judgments on my feet.

Ed: Thinking on your feet may be present, but what I'm talking about is something a little different. I'm talking about having faith in the idea that the right things will flow through the sieve that separates the conscious from the unconscious, and remaining alert enough to receive even a weak signal, and sensitive enough to yield to it. It's an attitude that could be characterized as when it gets through the sieve, I'll go with it. I'll yield to it. When it starts to flow, I experience it as flowing in sporadic spurts, the way water noisily gushes and spurts from a hose that was empty and connected to a faucet and is suddenly turned on, full force. I may intellectualize and analyze the intuition for some time. I may reflect on it, ruminate about it and massage it, before I have it in useable form. But I experience intuition as it usually happens much in this fashion.

Rich: I can identify with the process of yielding to intuition. And if you're asking how do you teach that process, I'd like to share what may be an insight with the panel. I had the experience of securing a major gift or contribution for my organization. I was subsequently invited to speak to a fundraising workshop on how to close on large contributions. It's embarrassing to say what I actually did do was prepare a whole presentation involving standard steps in the process of closing a donation. However, the way I actually work on closing a large contribution like that donation involves a series of intuitive insights and decisions which just come to me that have little to do with the so-called standard steps.

The simple fact is I don't know how to teach the intuitive part to other fund raisers.

Len: I have had similar experiences.

Annette: If I were trying to facilitate intuitive decision making I would put together some problems that the students would first take home the first week and try to solve intuitively; and then, take home a second time to solve in a more analytical mode.

Len: How would they do the exercises intuitively when they took them home?

Rich: Whatever felt good!

Annette: Have them go with it! For example, give them an assignment where they spend 45 minutes in an inward oriented state of relaxation of their own choosing, trying to become aware of what they felt would be a feasible solution. I've actually done this. About a year ago I faced the problem of what to do with my life for the next 5 years. I relaxed and meditated on this problem several times for about a week. One time while I was meditating, I experienced a mental image of myself riding through the countryside. What I remember most about this ride is that I was just sitting there letting life happen to me rather than trying to control my destiny. Now I am moving to Washington and I realize, perhaps for the first time, that the real reason I am making the move stems precisely from that meditation; namely, I will by this move let life happen to me. My unconscious goal was to let life happen to me more passively, like my experience of riding through the countryside was happening to me.

Ed: OK! I think that's an excellent example of the value of intuitive self-knowledge in a personal decision.

Rich: I'd like to share something with you that I find "weird" which happened to me about three years ago. One day I suddenly felt an urge to write poetry. I have never written any poetry before. I went with the urge and poetry started flowing out. It wasn't shabby. It was pretty good, at least that is what I was told afterwards. Over a period of about 3 weeks I composed over 40 poems.

All of a sudden I felt like doing it, and one night I stayed up all night. And then, suddenly, it turned off. After that time I couldn't seem to write a poem if you gave me all the dictionaries in the world. I haven't been able to write a single line of verse since then. I showed the poems to a number of people to see if they were any good. I got several offers subsequently to get them published. The poems were very meaningful to me, and this incident occurred at a crisis-like transitional time in my life when very deep feelings were being stirred inside me. But the experience has led me to believe that there is some type of creativity which can be switched on and off. It was switched on. I don't know how I switched it on, except I must confess it occurred during a stressful period in my life. It would be great for me if I could turn that switch back on again. I experienced the whole incident as weird, even a bit scary. I've never shared that before because I was afraid it would sound too strange.

Ed: On the contrary, Rich, I think it's quite relevant to what we're discussing. The poet William Blake is quoted as saying that on one occasion he wrote a poem "from immediate dictation, 12, or sometimes 20 or 30 lines at a time, without premeditation, and even against my will."[25] A. E. Housman reported that whole stanzas came to him "with sudden and unaccountable emotion."[26] These reports of things arising from the unconscious, full-blown and unbidden, though uncommon, are not rare. It seems that hard work and relentless logic does not enter until after the idea is discovered. Then it is linealized and sublimated.

[25] Colin Martindale, *loc. cit.*, p. 44.
[26] Ibid.

Bill: The great Russian composer Tchaikovsky is reported to have been often awakened from his sleep in terror by the sound of musical tunes only he could hear.[27]

Hal: Getting back to intuitive decision making as opposed to creativity.

Ed: I'm not altogether sure that they're entirely separate subjects, Hal. It may be that creativity is the fire sparked by intuition. Eric Fromm, in a book entitled *The Creative Attitude* says, "Creativity is the ability to *see*, or *be aware*, and *to respond.*"[28]

Hal: Well anyway, I think what we're talking about is how to turn intuition on and off for decision-making purposes.

Ed: Well, I still think there might be something else that is relevant in what Rich is saying. When that fire, or urge, arose inside, he yielded to it rather than try to label it, or ignore it. I think it is important to have decision makers understand that this cognitive function we call intuition does exist, and to at least experiment with yielding to it in less risky situations, until they build more self-confidence with its use.

I would like to address something that Rich alluded to earlier which related directly to this facilitation of intuition that we are discussing. In discussing how intuition works with several artists and writers I have frequently heard references made by them describing how they felt invaded or possessed by the creative insight as it emerged. They spoke of a process whereby an intuitive answer emerged at first at a scarcely perceptible level, and, as they identified with it and yielded to it, they felt eventually inflated by it, and finally possessed of it. They describe a feeling of being carried away by it, almost as if it was, just for an instant, con-

[27] Nina Berberowa, Tchaikovsky, (1941), pp. 204 and 212.
[28] Eric Fromm, *The Creative Attitude*, (New York: Harper & Row, 1960).

trolling them, rather than them controlling it. Now, I am sure its presence in intuitive decision making is a matter of degree. I would hardly expect it to exist with such dramatic form in everyday decisions. The people of whom I speak were directing their descriptions to decisions or problems of a more unusual nature. In addition, all of them described the habit of retreating to some quiet place, the studio by the ocean, whatever sanctum sanctorum provided quiet, in order to facilitate this process.

Len: It seems like this place where these people go to do intuitive deciding is being described as a place of safety where risk is extremely low.

Ed: Right, a place where they can be alone to indulge whatever eccentricities of style facilitates its expression.

Len: It seems I have to do that before I can open up.

Ed: And, therefore, what does that imply?

Len: That you have to teach people to go with that risk.

Ed: Yes, I think so, and to make it safe enough for them to experiment with intuition in order to encourage its development. It's very difficult to be intuitive in an intimidating environment.

Len: Yes, I think you can teach people how to deal with the fear and anxiety associated with that risk.

Annette: Yes. It's so important for a manager to do this with her people. It's just that so often there is so little time available.

Ed: I agree with that. Whether decision-making is being done on a group or individual basis, it must be safe enough for people to express in a nonjudgmental atmosphere what is coming through their intuition.

Bob: Yes, if you can set up a situation where you can encourage them to do what they feel is right and clearly communicate to them that you guarantee they're not going to lose on their next pay raise or otherwise on the job if they make the wrong decision. I think these processes can be encouraged to flourish. "Trust" is the essence of the problem here, as I see it!

Rich: That reminds me of something I was trying to say earlier. When you're in a position of substantial power and authority, from one viewpoint, there is very little risk.

Ed: Remember, there are two sources of risk. One is the risk of being criticized because your decision turned out to be wrong. This is a social risk. The other risk associated with intuitive decision making is the risk of acknowledging the power of the unconscious. The latter is a much more subtle, personal risk, and in some cases, much more potent. There may be much fear associated with the contents of the unconscious for some people, particularly when a person is bottling up something they are frightened will overwhelm them if it is released. Using a little poetic license, down deep we are all a little crazy, but many of us keep that hidden away—out of sight from others as well as from ourselves. Tales about creative, or intuitive people report that they are merely vessels for the Muse, who stampede through their brains and produce things whether they will it or not. While fascinating, folklore like this could also be a little frightening.

Annette: Aha! Yes, very interesting.

Rich: Right!

Ed: If we use the unconscious as a reservoir for problem solving, we risk the possibility of letting some of that crazy stuff float to the surface, which may be a little threatening. This may be an anxiety-producing stimulus that may be difficult to reconcile with one's adaptive role. In other words, you have to come to terms with some of your unconscious fantasies which may be bound up with vast amounts of psychic energy.

Bill: Tchaikovsky, in referring to the act of composing, said, "one forgets the whole world, becomes almost insane, all shakes and trembles within, there is hardly time to make notes."

Ed: So intuitive knowing may involve, at least sometime, a kind of subtle permission to risk losing control for a few minutes.

Rich: I think one way of facilitating this process is what usually passes under the title of brainstorming. The ground rule of brainstorming being, "say whatever comes into your mind, whether it makes sense or not," the object is to make the situation as safe as possible. Quantity is more important than quality.

Bob: Yes, and there has to be a lot of trust between people to make brainstorming effective.

Ed: Yes, Osborne's brainstorming uses the concept of deferring judgment in facilitating the flow of imagination. Edward De Bono has coined the term "lateral thinking" to describe this process in management.

six

How Can You Keep Stylish?

Manifesto for a Movement in a Mirror

Discarding rules as the tools of principal reliance,
preferring, instead, a unique and personal response
to a situation that is viewed in
its own uniqueness and novelty.

John R. Seeley,
Time's Future in Our Time

LEARNING OBJECTIVES

When you have completed this chapter you should begin to understand the following:

1. If we view the approach to decisions as either systematic or intuitive, many managers seem to favor the use of one approach over the other.
2. That this stylized approach to decision making is not absolute, but depends to some extent upon the other factors involved in a decision.
3. That we must, at least in the short run, take a decision makers personal style for granted.
4. More can be gained from enhancing a manager's decision-making style than trying to change it.

GLOSSARY

Pseudo-logical Falsely or spuriously logical. For example, a pseudo-logical model is one that looks logical on the surface, but upon more critical examination it is quite arbitrary.

Contingency Views of Management An emerging view or philosophy of management which is directed toward suggesting organizational designs and managerial strategies most appropriate to specific situations. The view stems from the realization that there is no "one best" theory of management.

We have observed a curious phenomenon that emerges frequently in mangement decision making. In cases where the decision maker has the latitude to use a more analytical approach or a more intuitive approach, many managers appear to move persistently in one direction or the other in addressing the decision. In other words, other things being equal (and of course they never are), managers often seem to prefer one approach over the other.

STYLES OF DECISION MAKING

There is some research to support this hypothesis. James McKenny and Peter Keen of Harvard University have reported considerable evidence supporting the theory that managers use different modes or styles when they solve problems or make decisions![1] Furthermore, they concluded from their research that there are two distinct types or styles of management problem solvers and decision makers. According to them, these different types are defined by the way the decision maker "thinks" and "organizes the data." One style is more logical, orderly, and analytical. McKenny and Keen describe this type of problem solver as "systematic." The other type or style they define is more heuristic, trial-and-error prone, or haphazard. This type of problem solver is described as feeling his way from one significant clue to another without a definite pattern of articulation based on a logical plan or rationale. The person simply gropes along, using intuition, from one clue to the next until a pattern emerges which seems to indicate a solution. The authors describe this type of problem solver as "intuitive." They report that the intuitive problem solver exhibits an ability to solve certain types of ciphering problems more

[1] James L. McKenney and Peter G. W. Keen, "How Manager's Minds Work," *Harvard Business Review*, May-June, 1974, p. 84.

"HUMM. I'VE GOT A VAGUE FEELING THAT PETERMAN'S ACCOUNTS SHOULD BE CHECKED."

quickly and efficiently than so-called systematic problem solvers.

McKenney and Keen also list what they feel are some important differences in the ways in which individuals with particular styles approach problems and decisions:[2]

[2] Ibid.

Systematic thinkers tend to:
1. Look for a method and make a plan for solving a problem.
2. Be very conscious of their approach.
3. Defend the quality of a solution largely in terms of the method.
4. Define the specific constraints of the problem early in the process.
5. Discard alternatives quickly.
6. Move through a process of increasing refinement of analysis.
7. Conduct an orderly search for additional information.
8. Complete any discrete step in analysis that they begin.

Intuitive thinkers tend to:
1. Keep the overall problem continuously in mind.
2. Redefine the problem frequently as they proceed.
3. Rely on unverbalized clues, even hunches.
4. Defend a solution in terms of appropriateness.
5. Consider a number of alternatives and options simultaneously.
6. Jump from one step in analysis or search to another and back again.
7. Explore and abandon alternatives very quickly.

The question that is most often asked is, which style of decision making is best? There is an old folktale which addresses this dilemma. It is the story of a wise old magistrate. During the hearing of a case, a plaintiff argued his side of the case so convincingly that the magistrate exclaimed, "I believe you are right!" The clerk of the court pleaded with him to restrain himself because the defendant had not even been heard. Then the magistrate was so impressed by the verbal eloquence of the defendant that he leaped to his feet and cried out as soon as the man had finished his presentation of the evidence, "I believe you are right!"

The embarrassed clerk of the court simply could not permit this; he indignantly begged, "they cannot both be right!" With an enigmatic smile on his face, the magistrate replied, "I believe you are right!"

The point of the folktale is that there is no one best process or style. No one style, systematic or intuitive, is universally appropriate for all managers or all decision situations. In the spirit of a "contingency view of management," the best style or combination of styles depends upon the nature of the decision problem, the type of management system, and a number of other factors that complicate the situation!

THE PERSONAL STYLE HYPOTHESIS

Some people do seem to lean more heavily on intuitive methods while others favor a systematic approach. William T. Morris enunciates what he calls his "personal style hypothesis": *More is to be gained from attempts to apply natural enhancements to the decision maker's personal style than from equivalent efforts to radically reformulate and externalize his style in the image of some pseudo-logical model.*[3]

According to this hypothesis we must take the decision maker's personal style for granted, as a point of departure, and then proceed to enhance it in order to make it more effective. For example, we would not try to force someone who favored an intuitive approach to radically shift to an analytical approach in decision-making. However, we might

---

[3] William T. Morris, *loc. cit.*, pp. 190-204.

encourage the intuitive person to develop analytical bases to validate intuition. By the same token, we would not try to coerce someone who preferred a systematic approach into scrapping the rationalistic approach in favor of unaided intuition. We would probably try to encourage the use of "gut feel" in those situations where the data gathered during the allotted time simply did not indicate clearly which alternative was definitely superior. The fundamental principle here is to *enhance* style rather than *change* it. Otherwise we may run the risk of seriously frustrating or confusing the decision maker and making him a less effective manager.

SUMMARY

Where a manager has the latitude to use either an analytical or an intuitive approach, many seem to use one approach more frequently than the other in their decision making. There is some research to support this "stylized behavior" hypothesis. More seems to be gained by attempting to enhance a manager's personal decision making style than attempting to radically reformulate it.

SKILL DEVELOPERS

1. Discuss the concept of "natural enhancements" in the *personal style hypothesis*. Explain more fully how this concept could be applied in the case of each style.
2. Try to rank everyone in your class or group as either a "systematic" or an "intuitive" decision maker on a 1–10 scale using 10 as "intuitive" and 1 as "systematic."
3. What hard data did you use in Question 2?

4. Explain more completely the meaning of the folktale of the magistrate in relation to problems of style in decision making.

5. How does the concept of contingency views in management relate to the *personal style hypothesis*? What are contingency views?

6. Decide whether you are systematic or intuitive! Then, using the attributes for systematic or intuitive thinkers listed in Chapter Six of the text, construct a simple analytic model of the type used in Chapter Four of the text to justify your decision.

PANEL DISCUSSION

Ed: I would like to introduce a concept that was briefly touched upon earlier in the dialogue. It is the concept of a manager's style of decision making. Pursuant thereto, I would like to read to you a quote out of an article in a text on decision making edited by Henry S. Brinkers which relates to this subject. The article, which is entitled "Matching Decision Making Aids with Intuitive Styles," is authored by William T. Morris, and I quote: "More is to be gained from attempts to apply natural enhancements to the decision maker's personal style than from equivalent efforts to radically reformulate and externalize his style in the image of some pseudo-logical model."[4]

Rich: In other words, don't try to change a southpaw pitcher into a right-handed pitcher.

Annette: Right!

Ed: If I have people working for me that feel comfortable with one approach rather than another, and they appear to be gaining success utilizing that approach, then I will try to enhance the style with which they feel more comfortable. Rich, if you tried to make Ken in your image, I'm sure he would probably experience a lot of hostility and anxiety, as I am sure would be the case were the situation reversed and you were employed by him. If we try to enhance a person's style, we may make him more effective. If we try to alter his decision-making style, we may run the risk of making him less effective. Before we conclude, I would like to ask each one of you, individually, what you perceive to be the decision-making style that you personally favor. We know that neither style fits all problems in all environments, but let us suppose that you have some latitude in approach possible. Which style do you think you would favor?

[4] Ibid.

Annette: I would like to lean more on the lineal or analytical approach to decision making. Time, pressure, and the pace at which I lead my life precludes it. There are so many things happening in my life that I realize I rely very heavily on the intuitive approach.

Hal: I guess I'll be a fence sitter and say I use each process about half of the time.

Bob: I use both the analytical and the intuitive processes every day; and I use them on the same problem. In making a decision as to what particular market segment will buy my new product, a number of factors might be evaluated and weighed against each other in selecting a specific sub-market. These factors might come out of an extensive marketing-research effort. Once the market is selected in such an analytical fashion, I might then use a very intuitive approach to creating the actual advertising copy used to capture the customer's imagination and increase the probability that he will buy.

Bill: I guess if you want numbers to describe the rational versus intuitive tradeoff in my decision making, it is probably done on about a 60-40 basis. Sixty percent being analytical and forty percent being intuitive. But it feels better to me when I make intuitive decisions. *I don't have to think I'm right; I know I'm right.* But even when I make intuitive decisions at work and I am asked why I made the decision I did, I cannot say that I do not know. I have to provide a justifying rationale for my superior in order to lend some credibility to my decision.

Len: I feel that between 85 and 90 percent of the decisions I make are primarily lineal.

Rich: I feel the majority of decisions that I make are intuitive. I also agree with Bill in acknowledging that when I make an analytical decision, I usually think I am right. When I make an intuitive decision, I usually know I am right.